Those Derby Days

*The Story of the Derby School
for the Partially Sighted, Fulwood, Preston*

THOSE DERBY DAYS

*The Story of the Derby School
for the Partially Sighted, Fulwood, Preston*

Garry Cheesbrough

Matador
9 Priory Business Park,
Wistow Road, Kibworth Beauchamp,
Leicestershire. LE8 0RX
Tel: 0116 279 2299
Email: books@troubador.co.uk
Web: www.troubador.co.uk/matador
Twitter: @matadorbooks

ISBN 9781788033596

British Library Cataloguing in Publication Data.
A catalogue record for this book is available from the British Library.

Printed and bound by CPI Group (UK) Ltd, Croydon, CR0 4YY
Typeset in 14pt Book Antiqua by Troubador Publishing Ltd, Leicester, UK

Matador is an imprint of Troubador Publishing Ltd

The Author would like to acknowledge the generosity of Galloway's Society for the Blind for funding the publication of this book during the year of their 150th Anniversary

Contents

Introduction

Although The School for the Partially Sighted, Preston (later The Derby School) opened its gates to children for the first time in 1945, my story will begin nearly eighty years earlier, during the reign of Queen Victoria and the Industrial Revolution.

The story begins with the formation of the Preston Industrial Institute for the Blind. There were many Blind Institutes scattered about industrial Britain but it was this charity that built and ran The Blind Homes at Fulwood in 1893 and it is this Victorian institution that evolved into a pioneering specialist school educating partially sighted children. The Preston Blind Welfare made the decision in 1944 to alter direction and oversee a new type of school.

From testimony of ex-pupils, I describe the first twenty years of this fledgling school as it struggled to meet the challenges of a new concept in education. Staff had to adapt from teaching the blind to implementing the revolutionary new methods in educating the visually impaired.

The next part of my story details the era of Ken Bridge, headmaster from 1965. Ken was highly respected for his energetic commitment to the school, setting in motion a vigorous programme of modernisation and initiating many new enlightened teaching methods and ideas. It was during his reign that the name changed to The Derby School.

In 1986, Ken retired and joined the campaign for the

school's continued existence against government policy, a battle that would ultimately be lost and see the school close its gates in 1988.

The final part of my story tells of the role the Galloway's Society for the Blind, the original Blind Welfare that started it all, played in organising reunions for ex-staff and pupils. The continued camaraderie that unites old school friends and helps long-lost pals "keep in touch".

"Sent to Preston"

A quick history of Preston from the perspective of the author.

Before I start my story, I want to tell you a little about the place where it all takes place. Preston is in Lancashire, in the north-west of England, and gained city status in 2002. I want to tell you a little about its history and characteristics of the (then) town that are important to the story of The Derby School.

 In 1969 when I began to hear talk that I may be "Sent to Preston", I had never heard of the place and when I asked about the town was told only that it was near Blackpool. Growing up in the West Riding of Yorkshire in the 1960s, over the Pennines felt like a million miles away. I was vaguely aware of the area from trips made to the coast. When it became certain I was going and the time approached, adults tried to sweeten the pill by telling me I was "Off to Preston, not far from the seaside!" In fact Blackpool is eighteen miles away and leaving home at nine years old for Derby School was no trip to the seaside.

At that time, it was policy that, once a local education authority identified a child as having some form of disability that impeded education, they should be referred to a special school that catered for educating that particular form of disability.

At Derby School I often went for walks round Fulwood, the residential district of Preston where the school was built. I noticed the old cotton mills, huge red brick buildings with tall chimneys, dominating the skyline like the paintings by L. S. Lowry. Derby School was born from the industrial history of the town.

The nineteenth century saw a transformation in Preston from a small market town to a much larger, industrial one, as the innovations of the latter half of the previous century brought cotton mills to many northern towns. These towns saw a sharp rise in population as people came from the surrounding neighbourhood to gain employment in the new factories. This influx of humanity created many new problems that the town's leaders needed to address, including housing and the welfare of the poor and disabled. As they struggled to come to terms with these massive issues, civil unrest and violence often erupted.

In 1842, a group of cotton workers demonstrated against the poor conditions in the town's mills. The Riot Act was read and armed troops corralled the demonstrators in front of the Corn Exchange on Lune Street; four workers were killed. A commemorative sculpture now stands on the spot. Inside that same building twenty-five years later discussions led to the building of the Fulwood Blind Homes, which later became the school that this history is concerned with.

This history of Preston is not unique; many towns were industrialised in the mid-nineteenth century and had charitable organisations that built institutions to house their blind and disabled. What makes Preston different is that the blind home they built was the first to convert to a school for the partially sighted in 1945. The Butler Education Act of 1944 forced other districts, some building from scratch purpose built schools like Exhall Grange at Coventry but while nearly every area had some form of mechanism to cater for the blind, facilities to educate this new category of disability remained rare and small scale.

While at Derby School, I experienced the town's celebration of the Preston Guild in 1972. This took place throughout the whole year and the children of the school were witness to many of the events that took place. These children will all have their own stories and memories of this unique event and it is probably the best example of how the town's character and industrial history affected the life of the school.

Henry II granted Preston's first Guild Merchant in 1179. The Guild was an organisation of traders. At intervals, the Guild Merchant updated its membership list. Anybody who claimed to be a member of the Guild had to come and swear loyalty to the Mayor. From 1542, the Preston Guild took place every twenty years. The rarity of the celebration, and the fact that large numbers of people congregated in Preston made the Guild a special opportunity for feasting, processions and great social gatherings. In this way the great festival which is the Preston Guild was born and continues to flourish today.

Preston has a strong Christian

(particularly Catholic) history and tradition, One of the proposed derivations of the name Preston is from 'Priests town' and the lamb on the city's shield is a biblical image of Jesus. The "PP" on the shield stands for either "Proud Preston" or "Princeps Pacis" (Prince of Peace). Going to church was a major part of school life. Pictured is Fulwood Methodist Church where children spent many a Sunday morning.

Preston as always been a major hub in the transport system of Britain, positioned on the River Ribble and an ancient highway. The town is also an important link in the rail network and possesses a huge Victorian station. The town also has an inland dock, the Albert Edward Dock, which opened in 1892. This was the largest single dock in the country. By the 1960s, the port held the record for handling the largest amount of container and ferry traffic and the school often organised trips around the docks. The Preston Bypass, now part of the M6, was the first motorway in Britain. When I visited the town centre for the first time I could not fail but marvel at the recently built bus station. In 1970, Preston had the biggest bus station in Europe. The futuristic-looking architecture had a huge impact on me; I had never seen anything like it. A new Guild

Hall also recently built and a system of subways linked the bus station, Guild Hall and town centre.

The more I discovered Preston the more I was bewildered by its sprawling diversity, which never failed to surprise me: Victorian monuments, the Harris Museum and Library 1891 sitting alongside the bright bold modernism of the Guild Hall and Bus Station, the genteel respectability of the streets of Fulwood punctuated by old cotton mills and canals, reminiscent of the brute force of industrialisation. The churches we attended, the parks we played in, the streets we walked along and the Preston Guild celebrations we supported, all contributed and coloured the background of the lives of children "Sent to Preston" and are a major part of the story of The Derby School.

1

The Fulwood Blind Homes

1893–1945

My story begins over one hundred years ago in 1867. Queen Victoria had been head of the British Empire for thirty years. A new government, led by Conservative Lord Derby, proposed to introduce parliamentary reform and further extend democracy. In the House of Commons, Disraeli planned a new Reform Act giving the vote to every male adult householder. Gladstone supported these proposals and the new measures became law [www. spartacus.schoolnet.co.uk, 2011].

In the north of England, far away from this pioneering work in London, in a town called Preston, a leading temperance organiser, Joseph Livesey, gathered together local dignitaries in the Corn Exchange on Lune Street to create their own piece of social reform. They were concerned about the plight of unemployed blind people in their town, many of whom wandered the streets as beggars. Attracted to Preston initially by the promise of work in the many cotton mills, they then found themselves on the streets and penniless during the 1860s as work dried up. To help combat this situation by providing the blind with work and training, they set up a charity: the Preston Industrial Institute for the Blind [Dean, 1987].

The predicament of the town's blind folk had pricked the public conscience during the early years of that decade, when the American Civil War had cut off supplies of cotton to the area's principal industry and left many with no means of supporting themselves. The institute's first premises were rented and a manager, John Catteral, and four blind workers engaged. Machinery and materials for making mats and brushes were purchased, but it was notable that even in those early days some time was set aside for education [R.G. Crawshaw, 2005].

During this period of British history, many blind institutes sprang up in industrial centres like Sheffield, Nottingham, Wolverhampton and Cardiff as they all encountered similar problems. For some towns it was their first experience of organised charity.

For the next twenty years the care and welfare of Preston's blind were an entirely voluntary effort. Donors included brewers Matthew Brown; grocers E.H. Booth, and Horrocks from the cotton trade. In 1872, one grand bazaar raised the incredible sum of £3,448. The money was desperately needed; there were no grants or subsidies from the government and the blind workers had to compete with other manufacturers to sell what they had made.

It had not slipped the notice of the government that blind people had a serious contribution to make to the economy and workforce of Britain. A Royal Commission was set up to investigate the education and training of blind people and the institute in Preston was selected for inspection [Dean, 1987 & R.G. Crawshaw, 2005].

The Commission was impressed and they recommended that the scope of their activities be extended to include much of Lancashire. In return for falling in step with government thinking, mandatory grants were made available to cover two-thirds of the maintenance cost of children who attended a special school for the blind. In 1893, the Preston and North Lancashire Blind Welfare Society, as it became known, purchased land on the corner of Lytham Road and began work on the building of the Fulwood Blind Homes, Preston. This building would be an elementary school for blind children and the headquarters of the Blind Welfare. This first building, which started with just two blind children, would fifty years later comprise part of what would become the School for the Partially Sighted.

The legislation that allowed this was the 1893 Elementary Education (Blind and Deaf Children) Act. This was one of the most important Acts passed for the benefit of the blind, and brought about the compulsory education of blind children from the age of five to sixteen. All schools for the blind were certified under Section 2 of this Act. The Act defined the word "blind" as "too blind to read the ordinary school books used by children" [M.G. Thomas, 1953]. This Act brought to public attention the need to direct funds towards provision for the blind and acknowledged that blind children could and should be educated.

Until this time of industrialisation, children with physical disabilities, such as a visual impairment, were not thought worthy of being educated because the impact they made on the economy was deemed insignificant.

In 1893, work began at Fulwood, Preston, on the corner of Lytham Road and Black Bull Lane. The 15th Earl of Derby was asked to officiate as guest of honour at the laying of the foundation stone, but in April of that year he died, so the duty fell to his widow, the Countess of Derby, and the Alderman W.B. Roper J.P. Chairman. The ceremony was held on 30th September 1893.

Two years later, in 1895, the Fulwood Blind Homes were formally opened by the 16th Earl of Derby and Lady Derby; the building cost £8,000. Lord Stanley of Preston had been Governor General of Canada but returned to England on the death of his elder brother.

In 1898, the institution extended the home to incorporate blind workshops, based on the cottage home principle, building on lower ground near Cadley Brook [M.G.Thomas, 1953]. This meant that the workshops were built as separate self-contained units at a distance from the main building. This system originates from the early part of the Industrial Revolution when craftsmen and skilled tradesmen began producing goods from their rural cottage homes.

In 1901, the glorious reign of Queen Victoria finally came to an end, and in Fulwood, the first Braille machine was purchased. A piano was also acquired to enable the boys to be taught piano tuning. No doubt the Braille lessons were as well received as they had been some eighty years earlier in Paris when Louis Braille's fellow pupils enthused about the "little system" he had developed. However, piano tuning proved to be a disappointment; most of the boys found that their wrists were unequal to the physical demands of the task at that stage of their development [R.G. Crawshaw, 2005].

The Second Boer War concluded (1899–1902), during which the Army Medical Corps discovered 40% of men called up for duty were physically unfit to fight. This led to the Liberal reforms of the first decade of the twentieth century. In schools, games and the minimum of one hot meal a day became compulsory. Like the reforms in nursing and patient care following the Crimean conflict, out of war comes a focus on helping the most vulnerable [wikipedia. org/wiki/Second_Boer_War, 2011].

After a school inspection in 1904, copies of the Preston Institute's instruction manuals were circulated to other blind schools across the country. Five years later the school extended its efforts by taking the benefits of education to a group of people who had hitherto been unable to share the experience. A teacher was engaged to visit and assist blind people who were confined to their homes. In 1909, that first year, more than 1,300 home visits were made and they opened up the world of knowledge to a large previously overlooked population [R.G. Crawshaw, 2005].

Within the school, progress was not achieved without occasional problems and not every pupil extracted the maximum benefit from the opportunities on offer. When a headmistress was appointed in 1911, mischief escalated into mayhem within a matter of weeks. By today's standards many of the preliminary incidents seem trivial and the punishments inordinately harsh: knitting needles broken, water spilt and choristers refusing to sing, but they were punished by caning and spells of solitary confinement which only led to greater disruption. The situation quickly moved out of control and extensive damage was wreaked on the school buildings. Doors and windows were broken, one smashed by a pupil wielding an iron bar. The fact that the perpetrators brandishing such weapons were unable to see the damage they inflicted must have served only to heighten the ugliness of the scene.

The culmination of such blind rage was a violent confrontation in which one of the older boys knocked the headmistress unconscious. Peace was eventually restored and three boys were immediately expelled. Following a period of sick leave, the headmistress also left the school and was replaced by a man. It is possible that the new head was selected because of a greater sensitivity to the pupils' needs, but there is no record of that. It seems more likely that he was preferred in the hope of imposing greater discipline [R.G. Crawshaw, 2005].

In 1913, a bequest of £5,000 was received by the Homes for the Blind, Fulwood, under the will of Alderman W.B. Roper, J.P., who had been present at the Blind Homes' opening. The sum of £2,000 was used for the erection of a boarding house and £3,000 for an endowment fund, but by the time the building was completed in 1914, the country was at war.

In the summer of 1914, Archduke Franz Ferdinand of Austria was assassinated; this triggered the beginning of one of the bloodiest conflicts in history: the Great War (1914–1918). Long-term causes, such as imperialistic foreign policies of the great powers of Europe, played a major role. Ferdinand's assassination by a Yugoslav nationalist resulted in a Habsburg ultimatum against the Kingdom of Serbia. Several alliances that had been formed over the past decade were invoked, so within weeks the major powers were at war; via their colonies, the war soon spread around the world.

More than nine million combatants were killed, due largely to great technological advances in firepower without corresponding advances in mobility. It was the second deadliest conflict in Western history. The first role for the new Roper Hostel was to supply the Red Cross Society with accommodation for nurses and up to thirty patients. However, the offer was not taken up and the new building was subsequently requisitioned by the army to lodge its recruits [Dean, 1987].

Over the next few years as blinded servicemen returned from the war there were many additions to the number of blind people who required help. Both funds and facilities again became stretched. Although the workshop's activities continued throughout the Great War, making baskets and hampers for use by the services, the possibility that blind men could make a direct contribution to the war effort was also recognised. In 1917, the National Air Board sought to attract a thousand blind men with what they hoped would be a highly developed sense of hearing, for use in operating anti-aircraft defences [R.G. Crawshaw, 2005].

After the war, the school continued to progress; knitting machines were purchased for the girls and boot and shoe repairs introduced as an additional activity for the boys. At this time, the management uncovered a rather dastardly deed in which a husband and wife team sold a donkey that belonged to the pupils. The couple, who had recently vacated the posts of superintendent and matron, pocketed the sum of two pounds after pretending the animal was their own. However, even with such distractions, no-one could deny the substantial achievements of the staff of the institute, and in 1920 they felt able to assure the Ministry of Health that there were no blind beggars on the streets of Preston. Every blind person who was capable of work was employed, either in the workshops or at home, using materials and equipment supplied by the Blind Welfare [Dean, 1987].

During the 1920s, the government devolved responsibility for blind welfare to the local authorities, but these bodies found it difficult to maintain the necessary funding during the years of the Depression. Voluntary assistance to the school by both individuals and private companies continued to be as essential as it had always been [Dean, 1987].

Eventually, in 1923, the Roper Hostel for Fulwood opened to perform its original purpose, nine years after it was built, designed to accommodate twelve blind men and twelve blind women [M.G. Thomas, 1953].

In 1930, ten men and nine women occupied the Roper Hostel, with forty-six in the elementary school, forty-three employed in the workshops, twenty-one trainees and eleven home workers. All together there were 537 blind persons on the register. The records of this time also state that two were otherwise employed [M.G. Thomas, 1953].

Thanks to the efforts and contributions of many people in the locality, the institute survived into the 1930s, when the economic picture began to brighten and the range of extra-curricular activities was widened again. Concerts and lantern-slide lectures were held on a regular basis; dancing, swimming and football were introduced, and Boy Scout and Girl Guide troops formed. The workshops also flourished, so much so that it was necessary to open a shop and put a sales representative on the road [R.G. Crawshaw, 2005].

Therefore, as the 1930s drew to a close, the Fulwood Blind Homes consisted of the original 1893 main building, which was the blind elementary school, the 1893–1898 blind cottage industry style workshops and the 1914 Roper Hostel. These were all red brick separated buildings within gardens occupying the land between Cadley Brook, Derby Road, Lytham Road and Black Bull Lane in Fulwood, Preston.

However, by the end of this decade the country was at war once more. The Second World War (1939–45) placed Britain and its allies once again at war with Germany. It was the most widespread war in history, with more than one hundred million military personnel mobilised. In a very short time, the country moved to a state of "total war", placing our entire economic, industrial and scientific capabilities at the service of the war effort, erasing the distinction between civilian and military resources. Marked by significant events including the Holocaust, the mass murder of civilians and the only use of nuclear weapons in warfare, it was the deadliest conflict in human history.

The last war had taken place in Europe and other countries far away, the Roper Hostel seconded and staffed to handle the consequences, caring for injured and blinded servicemen, and women in moderate safety. This conflict, however, had the frightening potential of inflicting danger and death upon everyone within their daily lives as Germany pounded our major cities with regular bombing raids.

The north of England, Manchester and Liverpool especially, were targeted for destruction, both large population centres with institutions for the blind. An evacuation programme was initiated.

The Preston school found itself sharing its premises with Henshaw's Institute for the Blind, which had been evacuated from Manchester. A reciprocal agreement was also reached with the Harris Orphanage situated nearby – if either premises were damaged by enemy action, the two organisations would share their facilities. The risk of attack by enemy aircraft meant there was no way of avoiding the effects of this war, though the installation of blackout blinds would have had less impact on the school than elsewhere. In the workshops, the demand for their services had never been higher and the repair of army boots became a major activity; sales figures broke all records [Dean, 1987].

It seems hard to believe that in the middle of this war, when the immediate must often have taken precedence over the important, the basis of the country's education and social legislation for the post-war era was being drawn up. The 1944 Butler Education Act became a major milestone that marked the pathway for a generation of children. Its inscription bore the commandment that children should be educated according to their age, aptitude and ability, and this was to include those with handicaps as well as those who were able-bodied [R.G. Crawshaw, 2005].

The Handicapped Pupils and School Health Service Regulations, 1945, established eleven new categories for the assessment of disabilities, and for the first time "partially sighted" was included and acknowledged as a disability for which appropriate provision would be made.

Once again, a war forced the conscience of the nation to focus on social reform, and this recognition between "blind" and those with sight, but not full sight – in other words, "partial sight" – was just one feature of a whole catalogue of welfare reforms to follow, once the conflict had concluded.

In implementation of this Act and in anticipation of the regulations to follow, the management committee of the Institute for the Blind in Preston confirmed to the Ministry of Education in February 1944 that it would be willing to function as a partially sighted school. Although the Preston Institute would still be responsible for the running of the school, it would be relieved by grants from the Department of Education and the payment of fees by local education authorities that sent their partially sighted children to the school. The blind workshops continued to operate, employing local blind people, but the vast majority of the buildings, including the Roper Hostel, would become a boarding school for partially sighted children [R.G. Crawshaw, 2005].

We will never know for sure why the committee decided in February 1944 to change policy from the care of the blind to educating partially sighted children, but we can make an educated guess.

During the war years, the trustees regularly liaised with other blind homes planning an accommodation strategy in case either institute was bombed. Throughout these talks, it would have become apparent how small scale the operation in Preston was, compared to the homes in Manchester and Liverpool. Figures stated in 1930 that Fulwood had sixty-five people boarding and thirty-two visiting daily using the workshops. At Henshaw's in Manchester, they had sixty-four residents, 194 workshop employees and 273 pupils [www.henshaws.org.uk/about/our-history.aspx 2010]. Preston would always trail behind these institutions when competing for funding.

The promise of new money and grants from government and local education authorities for this new category of disability would have been a major incentive for the Preston committee. Instead of competing with the larger institutions located in cities, they could operate as specialists in partially sighted education. This would create a completely new funding mechanism and help subsidise continued support for the blind. As a blind institute the committee's work would always focus on the local blind, but within that structure, they now had a school to run for the partially sighted.

At the end of the war, the evacuees from Henshaw's were returned, and the blind children of Preston were transferred to schools in Manchester and Liverpool. The Fulwood Blind Homes ceased to exist.

The elementary school building continued to house the main offices of the Preston and North Lancashire Blind Welfare Society, but around them, a new school for the partially sighted was poised and ready to offer visually impaired youngsters the specialised education that they had always needed but which had not previously been available [Dean, 1987].

2

The School for the Partially Sighted, Preston

1945–1965

On 3rd October 1945, just three weeks after the cessation of hostilities in the Far East, the *Lancashire Daily Post* announced that Preston had a new school [Dean, 1987]. The School for the Partially Sighted, Preston, with its first headmaster, Mr Fred Rothwell, became the very first school for partially sighted children in England, welcoming pupils from the whole of the north, the north Midlands and north Wales. [R.G. Crawshaw, 2005].

The decision by the Preston and North Lancashire Blind Welfare Society, as it was now known, to run a school for the partially sighted had major lasting consequences and defined the character of the school throughout its existence. This was to be a school run for the benefit of visually impaired children by people whose philosophy had only ever focused on the blind.

This ambiguity of purpose was clearly in evidence. This was still the home of the Blind Institute and the "Blind Homes" plaque was not removed or the home renamed. It is no wonder that for many people the school for the partially sighted was thought to be still a blind home.

The children resented the association with the blind; they regarded their sight as a kind of status symbol and did not care to be labelled as blind [R.G. Crawshaw, 2005]. This continued resentment by the children was just one of the lasting legacies created by decisions made at this very early stage in the school's life.

However, by far the most controversial decision that affected the daily lives of the children was the continued existence of the blind workshops in the school grounds near Cadley Brook. In those dingy sheds, men wove willow stems into baskets that would largely be sold to the local industrial market, and they both made and repaired cane seating. Shoe repairs were also undertaken, and a steady supply of boots and shoes was provided by the school for the local Fulwood army barracks.

Female workers made baskets, but most of their time was spent knitting a range of garments that included scarves, gloves, hats, sweaters and cardigans. The children were not encouraged to visit the workshops but when taking shoes for repair or retrieving a stray football they glimpsed the inside of these dark, dingy buildings, they didn't hang around long or wish to return [R.G. Crawshaw, 2005].

Although the school in Preston was the very first of its kind, many other blind institutes across the country soon followed in its wake to cater for partially sighted children. This model of a school running alongside blind industrial workshops was repeated elsewhere by other institutes like

St Vincent's in West Derby, Liverpool, a school for blind and partially sighted children run by the Catholic Blind Institute [/www.stvin.com, 2011].

Winston Churchill, who led Britain to victory during the war, found himself a member of the opposition when the election of 1945 returned Labour to power with a huge majority. Under the Parliament of Clement Attlee, the new government began some of the greatest changes in Britain's history, nothing less than a reconstruction of the nation. In addition, in Preston a new chapter began at the school for the partially sighted as it welcomed the first batch of disadvantaged children [www.lep.co.uk/news/ opinion, 2010].

Six classrooms built in a row, stretching from the hostel in a straight line along the bottom of the hill, were the only addition to the previous blind home's buildings. This was a very basic building with all classrooms leading outside. The only protection from the weather was a glass roofed, metal framed veranda. Building materials were in short supply just after the war so this would explain the elementary design. The first two rooms, to the left in this row were dedicated to the "juniors" or youngest children, being close to their accommodation in the Roper Hostel. The first was a playroom and their classroom (Class 1) was next door. Next came the tuck shop and school library, both

within the same room. Because of the scarcity of large print books, the library was very small and woefully inadequate. After that was Classes 2, 3 and 4. Class 4 was at the far end of the row, near steps leading up to the driveway. This was where the oldest children would be taught.

The school opened with four classrooms and took in about seventy boys and girls aged between five and fourteen, and being a new concept in education there were no specially trained teachers. The ones employed were a mixture of those with standard qualifications and experience, and teachers who had previously taught in schools for the blind, and this included head teacher Fred Rothwell.

The classrooms had an extra-large wall mounted blackboard with thick chalk, writing paper with heavy lines and desks with tops hinged at the front, allowing them to be angled upwards and tightened so pupils could bring work up closer to their eyes. The children themselves provided any magnifying glasses. Books were always in short supply, particularly ones with large print. The children were allowed access to Sharoe Green Library every Thursday evening, just up Black Bull Lane [www.lep. co.uk/news/opinion, 2010].

Just after the war, times were hard for everyone. Stringent financial measures, imposed to meet the enormous war debt, caused undue hardship. A fuel shortage severely curtailed exports, food was still severely rationed and in 1948 even bread and potatoes were rationed (both had been exempt during the war). By 1950, rationing began to be phased out, though not until 1954 was meat rationing abolished. It cannot have been easy to produce a well-balanced diet and keep within budget under these conditions, and this may explain some of the criticism the school's catering received during those early post-war years.

During the dark early days of the war, economist William Beveridge had put forward proposals for post-war "cradle-to-grave" social security. The government had taken on an emergency welfare responsibility; it provided milk for babies, orange juice and cod liver oil for children. It was now time for Labour to put the Beveridge Plan into full operation. Family allowances had already been introduced before the war's end. A National School Lunch Act was passed in June 1946. In 1948, the government introduced the National Health Service to provide free medical treatment for all. This was great news for parents of the partially sighted as their children could now claim free spectacles and child welfare services. Nationalisation of the hospitals made nationwide care available for the injured and seriously ill. The "Welfare State" had begun [www.britannia.com/history/nar20hist5. html, 2011].

Graham Crawshaw arrived at the Preston school from Yorkshire at the end of the Easter holidays, 1946, aged just seven and would remain for nearly eight years. He later returned to the school in 1973 as a childcare assistant. Being a pupil and a member of staff gave him a unique insight into the establishment. This is what he had to say about those early years:

Graham Crawshaw 1946-1953

'School life was as drab as the long, dingy corridors, where a recessed stripe at dado height was a hangover from the days when this was a school for the blind and the inmates used to feel their way along the walls. Just prior to my arrival, the school had been reopened as a specialist establishment dedicated to the education of partially sighted children, and it was the first of its kind in the country. However, for the first group of children

arriving there in 1945/46 there was little evidence that the school governors appreciated that vast difference between the needs of children with no sight and that infinitely more fortunate group that was learning to make the best use of severely limited vision.

'Those in that second category were able to walk down the corridors without reaching for the reassuring groove in the wall, but the drabness of the surroundings, which had been unimportant to the totally blind, suggested a lack of inspiration. How we would have welcomed a sprinkle of brilliant white gloss paint.

'Inspiration and imagination were similarly lacking in the school menu, which could have been something that would have attracted us all, regardless of our ability to see. We understood the realities of post-war Britain where the quantity of food was probably more important than variety and our situation may have been very little different from that of children in other boarding schools, but we certainly felt that we were a long way from home. The smells that permeated and lingered in the kitchen corridors always seemed stale, though they were clearly subject to some change. If they had not been, we could not have used them to identify the days of the week.

'Nevertheless, more detrimental than the drabness of our surroundings and the monotony of the diet was the ethos of the school. Fred Rothwell, our authoritarian headmaster, appeared to instil little hope of a brighter tomorrow in any of his charges. Poor sight would blight our lives forever and we should have to get used to it. When the history of this unique institution comes to be written, I trust that it will include some of the achievements of Ken Bridge and others who contributed to its transformation. I can relate only the memories of one pupil who lived through those early years, but I am happy to record that I survived the experience and like to think that I have made more of my life than Fred Rothwell led me to expect.' [R.G. Crawshaw, 2005]

In 1947, the government extended compulsory education to fifteen. This had been considered in 1939 but was delayed due to the onset of the war. The legislation was part of the Education Act of 1944 but did not take effect for three years. Michael Hartley was eleven years old when he first arrived that year. Here he reminisces to a local newspaper.

Michael Hartley 1947–1952

Michael has fond memories of happy, if strict, times at school and says that without the support and encouragement of its teachers he would not have developed his love of art, literature and music. The high standards of teaching at the boarding school also meant he could go on to college, enter a career in catering and work in the catering department of hospitals throughout the UK.

Michael remembers, 'On Guy Fawkes night a big display would be organised on the field at the back of the school, near Cadley Brook. We used to get big hampers of fireworks from the companies that made them. There were some enormous fireworks. A teacher used to set them off, but the prefects and the senior boys, of whom I was one, were allowed to set off some of them. We would discreetly hide a few away down our socks and the following night we'd have our own firework display. We had a fire escape off the dormitory and we'd open it up after lights out, with someone keeping watch, and have a little display on the escape.

'One year the watch shouted that someone was coming and we rushed down, shut the fire escape, put the lights out and got tucked up in bed. The door opened and a voice said, "What's going on here?" There wasn't a sound. One by one we got shaken, and we were all denying anything had been going on, and then we realised you couldn't see from one end of the dormitory to the other for smoke. We got the cane for that.'

One great thrill for the pupils was the year that Tom Finney, in those days a huge football star, came to the school as part of the Christmas festivities for a kick-about in the playground. Despite being a lifelong Blackpool fan, Michael said it was a real treat for them all. What was not such a treat was the regimented menu; if it was Friday, it was black pudding. If it was cheese and boiled beetroot, it was Tuesday [Singleton.E.1996].

Michael went on to say, 'In those early days the education was, to be honest, chaotic and inadequate. For many years, pupils, myself included, left with no qualifications whatsoever. It was no one's fault. It was merely the system. In its time, the principle was a good one, but it was ill thought through. That said, I loved my time there. Suddenly, after years of trying to compete with fully sighted fellow pupils I was competing on equal, if not better, terms. The problems of age and differing ability eased.' [www.lep.co.uk/news/opinion, 2010]

By 1949, the school needed to expand and accommodate more children, but materials were still in desperately short supply, so a special building licence was

needed for the alterations and extensions to be carried out. Those extensions meant the school was able to accommodate ninety-four children, and most of them were boarders who went home only at the end of term [Dean 1987].

This 1949 new building was the largest single building project ever to take place during the school's lifetime and would be very impressive. Eight new dormitories, seven accommodating four boys in each and one larger that could take six beds, were created, making space for thirty-four new male starters. There were far more boys than girls at the school and this new category of boys was referred to as "intermediates". The new "intermediate" dormitories branched off from a single central corridor. These rooms were smaller than the older dorms in the hostel and old school building, more like a bedroom than a dormitory. Each room had its own washbasin and the whole building benefited from central heating, a marvel at this time!

With a great deal more thought in design and layout than the original classrooms at the bottom of the hill, two new large teaching rooms occupy the ground floor of the new block. It is decided that the youngest children should be given the advantage of one of these modern, bright, spacious classrooms and the other given to a remedial class.

This new building joins the original school and the gym/hall together. Up to that point, the hall had been a separate building, previously part of the blind workshops. At the back of the hall is the laundry room and boiler house, tasked with providing all the hot water necessary for the new heating system. These rooms are accessed through the Boot Room and walkway round the back of the school stage. The stage is at the far end of the hall, and in keeping with the scale of these Victorian buildings is modest to say the least. 'I believe there used to be a church organ where the old stage once stood, but that was long before my time. It would have made a better sound than that tiny old Grand that Alice Smith used to bash the hymn tunes out on' [David Stanley Rowland, FB, 2014].

In 1950, the school had six classes. Class 1 (the "juniors") and Class 4 (a remedial class) are situated next to each other on the ground floor of the new block. Class 1 has a stairway leading down to the playground. Class 2 takes the room Class 1 occupied and at the other side of the school library, there are now Classes 3, 5 and 6. Besides being headmaster, Fred Rothwell also teaches the remedial class and makes this new classroom his main centre of operations. 'I think Mr Rothwell used Class 4 as his office. He always seemed to be on that old-fashioned typewriter bashing out letters for hours at a time' [David Stanley Rowland, FB, 2014].

Alice Smith from Kendal was Class 2 teacher throughout the 1950s, and another stalwart was deputy head and Class 6 teacher Donald Taysum from Gloucestershire. Here is what Michael Hartley had to say about him in a letter to the *Lancashire Evening Post* in 2010: 'He was wonderful… a near genius as far as I am concerned. Thanks to him, I finished up with a fairly competent understanding of arithmetic, technical drawing, art and problem solving. I also owe my lifelong love of literature and music to dear old Donald (Duck) Taysum. I cannot express in words how much I am indebted to him' [www.lep.co.uk/news/opinion, 2010].

This pioneering band of educationalists was tasked with the challenge of teaching during a time of changing attitudes towards the partially sighted. Prior to 1944, all visually impaired children – blind and partially sighted – had been educated as if they were blind. Now it was recognised and accepted that many had sufficient sight, and therefore it was necessary to educate them by sighted methods. The change could not have been greater; the whole emphasis would be on the use of the child's sight rather than the lack of it [R.G. Crawshaw, 2005].

The implementation of this change must have put enormous pressure on the teaching staff. In addition to the completely new task of teaching partially sighted children, they had to contend with the potentially daunting fact that their new charges were not a single-issue group but a random assortment of individuals, with widely different physical, medical and social problems, who were only loosely linked by the characteristic of poor sight. Even this was a very broad generalisation because no two children had the same type or degree of vision. There was variation

in long and short distance acuity and a wide range of response in relation to the direction and brightness of light. Compounding the difficulties of partial sight, there were children with other afflictions, including brain tumours, epilepsy, diabetes, heart problems, difficulties with mobility or speech, and psychological problems resulting from social deprivation, poor home and family circumstances [G. Crawshaw, 2005].

In the early years of the school there were no books available with large print but, when that deficiency was resolved, it was quickly realised that myopic children would need to have books with small print. As the years rolled on, evidence accumulated on other aspects: the importance of contrast, print density and line spacing. And as help was increasingly provided in these areas, it must have been rewarding to find that such attention to detail transformed the capabilities of children who in the past might simply have been classed as slow [R.G. Crawshaw, 2005].

Whenever children board within the walls of an institution, and this could be any institution at any age in history, their lively imaginations will invariably liken their predicament to inmates serving time in prison, and like a real prison, there will be escape attempts. During the time Graham and Michael were detained at the education authority's pleasure, bids for freedom were severely dealt with. Six to eight boys who climbed over the railings in the dead of night and were brought back by the police were flogged in front of the whole school and then expelled. There was no investigation into why they wished to leave. They had been sent to the school because it was the best place for them and if they did not like it, it was hard luck.

However, as this was the only school of its kind at this time, the punishment would potentially blight any prospect of future success [R.G. Crawshaw, 2005].

Children had to be fourteen before being allowed out of the grounds of the school unaccompanied and, even then, written consent from their parents was required. Until that milestone, a child's world was largely confined to the acre or so of land on which the school stood. Outside trips were supervised and children felt like zoo animals being given the opportunity to mingle with the public. Prolonged confinement inevitably resulted in frayed nerves and little irritations blew up into major quarrels [R.G. Crawshaw, 2005].

It did not help that the pupils were each known by number. Numbers were marked into all clothes. It was less trouble for the welfare staff to write numbers than names and they would have been larger and easier to see, but those numbers were universally hated. Identification by number seemed one more indignity that made the children feel different and not ordinary. Convicts had numbers and this just reinforced the feeling of imprisonment [R.G. Crawshaw, 2005].

Discipline was rather strict but in tune with the time. Staff expected to be respected and obeyed. Since discipline was the same for everyone, most considered it fair. Corporal punishment was an integral weapon in the maintenance of school behaviour and it was always applied to the hand, usually across the fingers for maximum pain. Offenders would take the blow as contemptuously as one could manage without changing expression or giving any indication of pain or discomfort. By reaching forward as the cane was struck, it was possible to take it on the palm of the hand, where there is more padding. One boy tried this but reached a little too forward and was hit on the inside of the wrist. He felt faint and had to report sick for the rest of the day [R.G. Crawshaw, 2005].

Generally, the school accepted the need for rules and most of the time the pupils would toe the line without question, even when there was no obvious point to what they were being told to do. There would always be staff that would abuse their position of authority and trust and use an excessive measure of control over the children. At the same time, other staff members would go out of their way to make life pleasant. Mr Higgins was unusual not only because he was a male member of the care team in a world of female welfare, but because he arranged midnight feasts for the boys. He would bring bread and dripping from a cafe in Preston he part owned, and after "lights out" and instructing the lads to be quiet, the feast would begin [R.G. Crawshaw, 2005].

The school was built on the side of a hill and the grounds ran down a steep bank to a little brook that separated us from sheep grazing in the neighbouring field. The field was owned by the school but often used by a local farmer. The field was preferred for sporting activities because it was flat and open. The playground was small and sloped [R.G. Crawshaw, 2005].

To get to the field, a sturdy wooden bridge with spiked railings on each side was constructed across Cadley Brook. The railings were there to prevent children falling in the water, but the spikes were a greater danger. A boy going down to the field to play football kicked the ball over the bridge; another tried to catch it and, reaching over the railings, impaled his arm on a spike. The damaged arm required attention from Matron and twenty minutes later, suitably bandaged, he was back to play the game [R.G. Crawshaw, 2005].

The stream used to flood its banks whenever it rained heavily and this was a regular occurrence, providing the children with much to write home about and excitement. Sometimes all the playing field would be flooded and resemble a lake, the water reaching right up to the limit of the school buildings.

At this time, the school term was organised very differently to a mainstream school. There were no half-term breaks. The children did not go home in February, at Whitsuntide or for the autumn potato-picking week. Those holidays were tucked on to the summer break. Consequently, the school terms were extra long, and so were the holidays. Many children believed they deserved a longer time at home to compensate for the seven-day week, but that was not the reason. However, the practical outcome of this resulted in the children not having anyone to play with once the local school reopened [R.G. Crawshaw, 2005].

To compensate for the extra long terms, the school arranged family visiting days. Family visits were allowed once a month; that would be about twice a term. On the appointed day parents could take their children out of the school and for the lucky few this would be a splendid family outing. The Lancashire coast was only eighteen miles away, with the multiple attractions of Blackpool almost within reach. For most of the pupils, however, visiting days would be more restricted affairs. Few parents could afford to run a car and so visits were circumscribed by the availability of public transport. For parents who journeyed many miles, the day would normally be spent in Preston; sometimes they barely moved outside the range of the school buildings. The important aspect of these visits was for the children to see their loved ones and so, even if nothing much happened, the children looked forward to them with eager anticipation [R.G. Crawshaw, 2005].

Once a year, around July, the school organised an outing, which usually took the children to Morecambe, Blackpool or the Lake District. Typically, there would be four coaches and a small army of welfare and teaching staff to cater for the needs of the hundred or so pupils. Once at the target destination, the children would split into small groups and scatter. The staff had the unenviable task of keeping an eye on all. Older pupils were allowed greater freedom and could explore the town unescorted so long as the children stayed together in small groups [R.G. Crawshaw, 2005].

About six or eight pupils lived in Preston and they came to school as day boarders. There were those that lived too far from school to be day boarders but near enough to go home each weekend. For those that were condemned to remain all term this group appeared very lucky, but everything is relative and most of these children had no knowledge of their good fortune [R.G. Crawshaw, 2005].

The remainder, who were there for the duration, had only the monthly parental visit to break up the lengthy period between holidays. Going-home day never came fast enough and during the final week of term the anticipation of release built up steadily. The final night before going home was called "rubber night" by staff, who found the children continuously bouncing out of bed and unable to sleep, such was the excitement. These high spirits often led to mischief and it became something of a ritual to play practical jokes on one another. The most popular was the "apple-pie bed". Despite its predictability there was always someone who would be caught out; a child would jump into bed when the duty teacher came round to quell the noise and put both feet through the sheets that had been turned back halfway down the bed. Hopefully, by the time the ripped bed linen was discovered the culprit would be half way home [R.G. Crawshaw, 2005].

Travel to and from school was organised and paid for by the local education authority. Staff from the education department would escort the children on their journey. For long distances, this was invariably by reserved seating on a train. In the 1950s it was still possible to travel third class so this was a rare privilege, but the children simply saw it as another difference between them and "ordinary" kids, so didn't appreciate it [R.G. Crawshaw, 2005].

Here are the memories of Llewellyn Sadler, another little boy sent to Preston in the '50s, aged eight years old. He was following in the footsteps of his older brother Alan, who had already been at the school two years:

Llewellyn Sadler 1950–1958

'When we were in the infants we used to go to bed at 6pm and just when we had got off to sleep, Miss Fox, the attendant, would waken the whole dorm and make us line up outside the toilet and stand and listen to see that we had a pee! This was to prevent bedwetting. We were all standing there, falling asleep on our feet.

'The night before the end of term in the intermediate block we used to go into the Slush Room, get the polishing gear and a gang of us would polish the long corridor, then put on our clean socks that had been put out ready for going home, then one of us in turn would take a run and slide down the corridor while the rest of us would clobber them with pillows as they slid past; not many made it to the end!

'In wintertime we spent many hours, after lights out, sitting on the heated towel rails in the middle of the dorm in the intermediate block, telling yarns and fooling about.

'The dentist who visited the school was a Mr Douge, nice man, but feared by all. After his visit Mr Rothwell would announce at assembly the four names who needed to go to his surgery in town and Mr Douge would pick them up in his car and return them to school afterwards.

'The optician was Mr Mellor; what a great chap he was. I think his shop was in either Fishergate or Lune Street, I'm not sure. Mr Mellor had a clubfoot, but I never heard anyone take the mick, you know what kids can be like. Our music teacher was Miss Caulson. She was not a member of staff but used to visit the school to give lessons. It was always a fight between us lads as to who got to clean her car for a tanner. The gardener was a chap we so cruelly called "Dummy" because he was deaf and dumb. We used to watch mesmerised as he cut the lawn outside classes two, three, five and six. He used a big petrol mower, not

33

a sit-on one, and as he was only tiny it used to whip him round so fast when he got to the end of a run that it made us all laugh, even Mr Taysum!'

Describing the accommodation, Llewellyn says, 'I marvel at some of the changes to the school since I left. I have seen in some photos that there were carpets on the floor, something we never had. The toilets in both the senior and infant Blocks had glazed windows; they were open in my day with bars for security. In the hostel building there were the kitchens and dining room. In the dining area on the wall, facing the entrance door was a small wood and glass trophy cabinet that held the "House Cup", competed for each year by the house teams.

'If you walked through the dining hall and swing doors, on the left was Mr & Mrs Rothwell's private sitting room. Further down was the surgery; outside the surgery were the stairs leading up to the girls' dorms. There was one room up there that was used as an isolation ward when any child needed to be kept away from the rest of us if ill.' [L. Sadler, email, 2014]

Although they had a sitting room within the school, the Rothwells lived in a bungalow conveniently situated near the school. It was across the field opposite the bridge.

For any young child first arriving at the school, the number of staff and their different responsibilities would be confusing. Being a boarding school there were two teams of staff: the headmaster and his teachers and the matron and her childcare assistants, or "attendants" as they were known at this time. These two groups would work closely together and responsibilities merged, with the headmaster being in overall control and having the final word. Apart

34

from the teaching staff, the biggest influence on a child's day-to-day life would be Matron.

The school's first matron was Matron Heath. She was very keen on giving the children a dose of Epsom salts every Friday morning at breakfast. Graham remembers her being a large square woman who wore a perpetual frown and never appeared to smile or enjoy a joke. She was starched and formal, every bit the stereotype of a school matron. She brooked no argument, having the certitude that is available only to those with limited knowledge. When a child had a boil, she snipped off the top with scissors and squeezed, and if you had a sore throat, she would paint it with iodine. One did not go to Matron with minor ailments because the cure was generally less comfortable than the problem itself [R.G. Crawshaw, 2005].

In 1951, Matron Heath retired and was replaced by Matron Berry, a younger woman whose kindness was at once more obvious and more recognisable than her predecessor's. In her training, the new matron had been exposed to more enlightened medical thinking, and after taking one look at the Friday morning preparations, she insisted that every mug of the foul Epsom salts be poured down the sink [R.G. Crawshaw, 2005].

There was also a Matron Sumner with attendants Miss Fox, Miss Cusak, Mr Craig and Mr McNoughton [Llewellyn Sadler, FB, 2014].

Each well-regimented day began at 7.30am with a strip-wash. It was a little primitive, but at least there was hot water. The washroom was unheated and the stone floor was freezing. Breakfast was satisfyingly filling if a little monotonous; porridge was followed by bread and jam or marmalade. In the immediate aftermath of war we knew that food was strictly rationed outside as well as inside the school and we never felt disadvantaged [R.G. Crawshaw, 2005]

	1955
Class	**Teacher**
Class 1	Mrs Littlewood
Class 2	Alice Smith
Class 3	John Law
Class 4 (remedial)	Fred Rothwell (Headmaster)
Class 5	Edwin Lees
Class 6	Donald Taysam (Deputy Head)

After breakfast, the children returned to the dormitories to make their beds and brush their teeth, watched over by the care attendants. The school day began, as it would finish, with a formal assembly where a hymn that had been learned by heart the previous week was sung. The school had no large print hymnbooks, so the timetable included one period each week that was specifically set aside for learning the hymns [R.G. Crawshaw, 2005].

After assembly, lessons began. At 10am, there would be a short break and then lessons resumed until 12 noon. Then we could enjoy the luxury of a two-hour lunchtime. The lunch would be filling but predictable; one day would be sausage; another, Lancashire hotpot and then it would be stew. On Fridays, it was always fish. It was possible to tell the day of the week by the menu [R.G. Crawshaw, 2005].

Afternoon lessons stretched until four, but there would be an additional "activity" hour between six and seven. In between, we would have tea, black treacle, jam, potted meat, fish paste or brawn. After tea, we would put on our "play clothes" and then clean our shoes ready for school the next morning [R.G. Crawshaw, 2005].

The activity periods were aimed at broadening our education, but they also served to keep us out of mischief another hour. Dancing and music appreciation were included in addition to "prep" and in some sessions the duty teacher would read to the senior school from a range of suitable books. In summer, the activity hour was usually spent outdoors engaging in a range of sporting activities that would be familiar to any school. We played cricket, rounders, netball and volleyball, with no concession made for our imperfect eyesight. I suspect we played all these games to a relatively low standard, but there was no one with whom we could compare and we enjoyed them nonetheless [R.G. Crawshaw, 2005].

Given the choice, however, most of us would prefer a game of billiards or snooker. Played on a half-size table, we found these games so much easier because the balls remained stationary until they were struck. Our enthusiasm for these games can be gauged from the fact that we regularly organised tournaments and awarded handicaps to individuals according to our assessment of their visual difficulty. The school did not regard these games as appropriate for the formal activity hour, but we still enjoyed them [R.G. Crawshaw, 2005].

After an hour of that, it was back to the dormitory for half past seven and lights out at nine. However, before the day was complete we had to undergo our strip-wash again and get ready for bed. In the little time that remained, we were encouraged to read our own books, but this was not popular because of the difficulty seeing the print. The time just before lights out was the nearest the children came to a Happy Hour; if any mischief was going to occur it was during this precious free time [R.G. Crawshaw, 2005].

Once a week during the summer term we would go swimming. This was accepted as an important part of the school day rather than an evening activity. We were taken to the main swimming pool in Preston and given lessons by one of the instructors. It was popular with the pupils and no special treatment was given [R.G. Crawshaw, 2005].

At weekends, we were regularly taken on organised walks in the surrounding area of Fulwood. This part of Preston was considered safe for the whole school to be conducted along the public highways in a long string of pairs, before we broke up into less organised groups when we reached the fields and parks. If the weather was really foul, an indoor alternative would be arranged; but if it was merely wet, we would not be deterred from our usual walk and the rain would not prevent us from enjoying our short break outside the grounds [R.G. Crawshaw, 2005].

Sunday morning meant church and that would be Church of England. Attendance was compulsory and no one was ever asked whether our families owed any allegiance to any other denomination. For the children it was another opportunity to sing the hymns learnt at school. Then, before we knew it, it was Monday morning again and we were back to the weekday grind [R.G. Crawshaw, 2005].

The range of subjects was not any narrower than that covered in ordinary schools, but there were differences in teaching style and inevitably in the rate of progress. Class size was small with normally sixteen pupils arranged in four rows of four. This meant that no one was ever far from the blackboard and if anyone needed to take a closer look they were encouraged to do just that. When the new teaching block was completed in November 1949, it included large windows on both sides and these ensured maximum benefit from natural light. In many subject areas, memories were exercised in place of the written word with the aim of reducing any strain on the eyes. That also gave the whole class, encompassing a range of eyesight from poor to very limited, more of an even chance to learn and to demonstrate their knowledge. When thoughts had to be transferred to the page, this presented severe difficulties. Despite the use of lined notepaper with one–inch spaces between the lines, some children still struggled to write in the intended areas [R.G. Crawshaw, 2005].

Such children were on the borderline of acceptability for the school and the worst affected were eventually transferred to Henshaw's in Manchester, a school that catered for children who were blind or near blind. Happily, there were other children whose sight improved and they moved in the opposite direction from Manchester to Preston. A number of pupils had previously attended a school for the blind and these children were notable as the only ones who knew Braille. At Preston, it was not the policy to learn Braille but to make the most of the sight a child already possessed. This transfer between different types of school is clear evidence that the Lancashire authorities were attempting to look at the individual's needs by providing the appropriate learning environment. There were even a few children whose sight improved to the point where they could be sent to an ordinary school [R.G. Crawshaw, 2005].

English lessons included a good deal of reading aloud and poetry recitation; there was composition, dictation and spelling too. The children's abilities were regularly tested in the letters written home every week, which were produced in class as part of the formal curriculum. English literature consisted of stories read aloud by the teacher, followed by more limited and less literary attempts to put the story down on paper. Children were encouraged to read individually at their own pace and to make use of the school library, but they had to struggle with the fine print. The school library had no large print books and the reading aids provided gave limited assistance as the double convex lenses on a stand distorted the print [R.G. Crawshaw, 2005].

Arithmetic was treated in much the same way as English, with oral practice replacing bookwork. Tables were learned and practised by rote; in Year Two, the first ten minutes of every day were spent reciting timetables almost like a chant [R.G. Crawshaw, 2005].

Music was probably the ideal subject for children with visual problems since they could pursue a normal curriculum without undue difficulty. There was a healthy element of singing in class time and many of the children sang in a choir, sometimes linking with other schools to form a massed choir. Christmas and end of term concerts always attracted municipal support, with the town mayor usually attending [R.G. Crawshaw, 2005].

Music classes also included percussion bands for the young pupils and a recorder band for the seniors. All these lessons were held in the hall/gymnasium, which until the building of the new block had been a separate building and this avoided significant disruption to the rest of the school. The music teacher, Miss. Hurst, also offered piano lessons as an extra option [R.G. Crawshaw, 2005].

One musical event that stands out was participation in the celebrations of the 1952 Preston Guild. These Guild celebrations were held in the town every twenty years. In Graham's final summer at Preston this event was honoured by a visit from the Queen; it must have been one of her earliest visits following her coronation in June. The BBC broadcast the performance [R.G. Crawshaw, 2005].

The curriculum also covered other subjects such as history, geography and the concepts of algebra and geometry. A little biology, physics, PT and art were also studied. Religious study also took its place in the timetable and involved a fair amount of reading from the Bible. The Bible kept in the hall for assembly was the only large print book in the school. There were practical lessons too and these activities were drawn up strictly along sexist divisions. The boys did woodwork and a little technical drawing, while the girls learnt knitting and raffia work. In 1953, this attitude was common practice and none of the children ever showed an interest in the other subjects [R.G. Crawshaw, 2005].

Sports Day was similar to that of most junior schools. Parents were invited to attend if they were able to spare the time midweek, but they never formed a large crowd. Some events proved more difficult than may have been the case elsewhere. The egg and spoon race commonly turned into "find the egg", and no one insisted that competitors should start and finish with the same egg. The obstacle race was hardly novel when pupils could be relied upon to find obstacles everywhere. The cross-country race was held entirely within the school grounds, since the children rarely went out of the gates without a guide [R.G. Crawshaw, 2005].

To add competitiveness to proceedings, the schoolchildren were divided into house teams with their own colours. These were named after the saints: Andrew, David, George and Patrick. David Rowland Stanley remembers being captain of St Andrew for a while, 'but we never seemed to win anything!' Teacher Alice Smith was team leader of St Andrew with Brian Turner, St David; Noel Jones, St Patrick; and Donald Taysum, St George [David Rowland Stanley, FB, 2014].

Throwing the javelin, discus or shot was also considered potentially dangerous and was substituted with throwing the cricket ball and kicking a football. These may have been rather tame alternatives, but at least no one was speared or felled by a heavy object. One feature of Sports Day that encouraged both interest and involvement was prize money: sixpence for third place, a shilling for second and two shillings for the winner. This prize money was a welcome supplement to the children's pocket money [R.G. Crawshaw, 2005].

Postal orders sent to the school were credited to each pupil's account for purchases that would be made in the school tuck shop. It was a convenient arrangement that avoided the problem of lost coupons, a continual worry in the days of rationing, and since children were not allowed out of the grounds to visit other shops the tuck shop was the only choice. Government-enforced retail price maintenance meant prices were the same as shops outside the school. The shop was open only twice a week and sweets were restricted to two ounces on one day and four ounces on the other; it was not even sufficient to worry the school dentist. It was perhaps fortunate that those attractive items were restricted because the children's pocket money was needed for necessities too, like toothpaste, combs and shoe polish [R.G. Crawshaw, 2005].

If the school was deficient in any area, it was the lack of preparation for the outside world. The school governors failed to recognise that preparation for life needed to be better than that obtained by the average pupil in an ordinary school. In the wider world, the children needed something to compensate for their additional difficulties. Most of the day was spent in the same class, with no segregation into groups that could move forward at different speeds. The only concession to differences in learning ability was the existence of "Class 4", which was reserved for those who were having difficulty keeping up; this class was jumped by most. There were no pretensions towards higher education, qualifications or external examinations. The mood at the time was that these children were handicapped and not too much should be expected [R.G. Crawshaw, 2005].

Graham left the School for the Partially Sighted, Preston, after nearly eight years, at Christmas, 1953, two months after his fifteenth birthday; and as he struggled in the real world to find gainful employment without any recognised qualifications, fighting prejudice and ignorance, the school continued its work.

Freda Wood (Miss Shepherd)
Class 1 teacher 1957-1985

'The picture that Graham paints of life at school in Preston is exactly the same as the one I found as a young teacher when I first joined the staff in 1957. It was a tough, miserable regime with little to relieve the monotony and no compensations for children who missed out on all the joys and advantages of a caring family environment. There were times when I thought of leaving to find more satisfying, less frustrating employment – but how glad I am that I didn't. It was wonderful in later years to see the children given both encouragement and opportunities to achieve their full potential in the outside world.' F. Wood [R.G. Crawshaw, 2005].

The year Freda Shepherd arrived at the school, Evelyn Webb, who had taught Class 3 since 1955, left to work in Canada but returned a year later to marry her colleague Donald Taysum and settle in Preston. Up to that time Mr Taysum had boarded at the school. The couple had a daughter Elizabeth (now Liz Minton) and here she relates some of her own and her mother's memories of the school:

'My dad used to teach the older children maths, English, art, woodwork, and some technical drawing. My mum says the matron was a really unpleasant woman and should never have been caring for kids. The very young ones she used to put to bed at about six o'clock. The evening meal consisted of bread and margarine with a teaspoon of jam every night. She said the teachers used to do boarding duty at weekends on a rota basis (two teachers at a time – she remembers doing the rota with my dad and thinks that is how they got together). Saturday mornings used to be a visit to the cinema club in town, afternoon a compulsory walk, Saturday evening was social time – playing records, dancing, etc. Sunday morning was church, afternoon another walk, Sunday evening was story time. After work, the matron used to take over and my mum, dad and Alice Smith used to go for a drink in the Plungington pub opposite the school.

'My dad's father also used to come up from Gloucestershire to stay with him at the school from time to time. I felt strongly associated with the school, probably because of the strong association to it of my dad. I used to visit quite frequently during the '60s, especially at Christmas time, when my dad used to write and direct the school play.

'As a child and an outsider I thought it was a wonderful place, but my mum told me later that at the time she taught there in the '50s, there was a lot of unhappiness: young kids away from their families, and the house mistress (not sure if that's the correct term) sounded like a particularly callous, unpleasant sort of woman. She wasn't very nice to the kids at all, and my mum was shocked at the quantity and quality of food on offer. I never got the chance to find out my

dad's opinion of it. Alice Smith, Class 2 teacher and friend of my parents, died a few years after my dad, when she was staying with us as it happened. She had similar opinions to my mum; she said many of the kids were very unhappy. I think, hope, it changed a bit as the years went on and life became a bit better for pupils there.

'I remember my dad being quiet and strict but fair. I hope he was the same with his pupils; I could not fault him as a father. He was an old-fashioned sort of gent. Used to chain-smoke, later smoked a pipe (that is how I remember him).' [Liz Minton, FB, 2014]

During the same year (1958) that Donald and Evelyn were married, the blind workshops were doing a roaring trade, selling £87,000 of goods annually, but cheap foreign imports soon began to affect sales [Dean, 1987].

Mary Neary comes to work at the school as part of the childcare team in 1961. Like many of the welfare staff, she lived nearby in Fulwood, in fact, just across the road from the school and was based in the hostel caring for the infants or "juniors". She witnessed the last few years of Fed Rothwell's regime and remembers him and his wife at the school: 'The couple didn't cut a picture of what you would expect; Mrs Rothwell was never seen without a cigarette in the corner of her mouth and walked round the school in her slippers.'

Her fondest memory was of how attached the little ones could become, some even calling her "Mum", but she always reminded them they had a mother waiting for them at home. Others best remember Mrs Neary for her lively sense of humour and very loud laughter during the school's concerts and shows.

Also in 1961, one of the school's longest serving and founder member teachers, Alice Smith, retires. She returns to Kendal via Kent Bank and continues to keep in touch with her friends at the school [Liz Minton, FB, 2014].

After Alice Smith left, Class 2 had a succession of teachers: first, Miss Goodwin and then Mrs Best and then Miss Ludden, all lodging at the school in the flat at the senior girls' end. Eileen Berrisford remembers Mrs Best, who was really great: 'I think she must have been ex-services because she was so regimented, but what great fun. She lived in the senior girls' end and was The BEST' [E. Berrisford, FB, 2014].

1965 and a new matron arrives, residing in the hostel and taking charge of childcare. After twenty years in the job, Fred Rothwell announces he is to retire.

	1964
Class	**Teacher**
Class 1	Freda Shepherd
Class 2	Miss Goodwin
Class 3	Brian Turner
Class 4 (remedial)	Fred Rothwell (Headmaster)
Class 5	John Robinson
Class 6	Donald Taysum (Deputy Head)

3

The Derby School and
the Impact of Ken Bridge

1965–1977

After twenty years the school's first headmaster Fred
Rothwell retired and in September 1965 the school's
governors appointed Kenneth Bridge from Bolton in his
place. Ken made the short journey from his previous post
at the Harris Orphanage in Fulwood [Mrs M. Neary, 2010].
Under his leadership the school would gradually steer itself
in a new direction with an enlightened philosophy.

It was clear the committee of the Blind Institute,
who made the decision twenty years earlier to focus
their attention on the partially sighted, had no real idea
concerning the different nature of this disability or the
different teaching methods necessary for success. Quite
understandably, as this was a new concept at the time, they
had completely underestimated the challenge ahead.

As Graham Crawshaw's testimony in the last chapter
explains, the school continued almost as before like a
home for the blind. Accommodation was increased along
with other changes, but the culture was one of generally
treating the children as partially "blind" rather than partially

"sighted", with an emphasis on what the child could not achieve rather than what they could. However, it was not just staff philosophy that needed to change; if the school was really going to move forward, sources of new investment were necessary. The money that came in from government and the various local education authorities clearly needed supplementing.

Maybe it was with all this in mind that the governors appointed Ken Bridge. If the culture of the school needed to change, it would come from the top down. Ken was known by the members of the school's board from fundraising events they had all previously attended, and it may well have been partly Ken's experience in raising money that helped him secure the job.

His approach was to liberate the school from many of its old traditions and rules, encouraging the children to be more independent and allowing greater freedom. He instilled confidence and saw beyond the visual disability of his charges. He had a unique talent for unearthing the hidden potential within his students and encouraging them to reach heights, which surprised even themselves.

Ken was a member of the Preston branch of the Rotary Club, an organisation dedicated to helping others. Members gave their time and talents to serve the local community and share a common interest in helping others [www.ribi.org/about-us/what-is-rotary, 2011].

Through this association, Ken had access to a valuable network of business people and professionals who were experienced fundraisers. In exchange for allowing the school to host Rotary Club charity events, many such functions were arranged that created valuable donations for the school.

Since the early 1960s the school had held regular reunions for ex-pupils, and a major issue of concern repeatedly raised was the negative impact the name of the school had when filling in application forms for job vacancies. This feedback is noted and the school's name is changed [Llewellyn Sadler, FB, 2014].

From 1965 the school becomes the **Derby School**, a big step forward that cost very little but signposted the way ahead. "Derby" was chosen because of the association with Lord and Lady Derby stretching right back to the opening of the institution in 1893. Importantly, it didn't create any preconceived ideas about the applicants who attended such a school. This change in name comes about just as Fred Rothwell retires, so when a new sign is commissioned it shows the name of his replacement.

Unlike his predecessor, Ken was to dedicate all his time to the responsibilities of headmaster and only teach informally, so a new teacher, George Gooch from Norwich, is appointed to take over the remedial class. With his eccentric character and boyish enthusiasm for all things scientific and mechanical, Mr Gooch would make a huge contribution to the lives of pupils in and out of class. The tuck shop is closed down and in that small room at the back of the reference library, two desks and a filing cabinet are squeezed in. For the first time the headmaster has an office! The second desk is for his secretary.

In 1966, Labour win the general election and England are crowned World Cup champions. In the blind workshops, the repairing department closes, no longer commercially viable, and a young Ruth Collins joined the school childcare staff, becoming deputy to the new matron, Veronica Miroscoe. She will mainly be responsible for the youngest pupils accommodated in the hostel. Miss Collins became the friendly, sympathetic face of childcare, opposed to Matron, who was unapproachable and generally disliked by the children, so much so that they nicknamed her "Hitler", but never to her face.

Miss Ann Regaud – pronounced "Reego" – from Freckleton joins the teaching staff, taking Class 3. Shortly after joining the school and the children mastering her name, it changes when she marries Chris and becomes Mrs Ann Colbert. Ann taught French and went on to become a very popular teacher. Because of her love of Tolkien, she introduced a generation of children to the exciting

Headmaster: Ken Bridge	1967
Class	**Teacher**
Class 1	Freda Shepherd
Class 2	Miss Ludden
Class 3	Ann Regaud (Colbert)
Class 4 (remedial)	George Gooch
Class 5	John Robinson
Class 6	Donald Taysum (Deputy Head)

adventures of Middle Earth with her readings of *The Hobbit* and *Lord of the Rings*.

John Robinson is Class 5 teacher. John Blain remembers, 'He used to save pupils money on fountain pen cartridges by refilling them from a bottle of ink using a needle and syringe, which he probably got from his wife who was a phlebotomist at Preston Royal Infirmary' [J. Blain, FB, 2014]. Donald Taysum, ever present deputy head and Class 6 teacher, is now the only link back to the school's earliest days.

This decade was labelled the "Swinging Sixties". With the '60s came a liberated attitude, ready to rebel against the political and social conservatism which had gone before. The new young generation wanted its freedom. Newly affluent, it created a huge explosion in the market for rock and blues, with bands emerging such as The Doors, The Jimi Hendrix Experience and Janis Joplin – many heavily influenced by the psychedelic drug culture which came with the hippie movement [www.bbc.co.uk/britishstylegenius, 2014].

Teenagers dream of forming their own bands and gaining fame and fortune like the Rolling Stones and the Beatles. The older children at Derby School aren't immune to this trend. Here, Eileen M. Berrisford gives a brief history of the Derby Diamonds, the school's own pop group. 'It must have been January 1967 when the group was put together by a guy named John Worrell, who would come into the school on a Tuesday night to teach some boys the guitar. It then transpired to form a folk group to help the lads get more practice. The original line-up was: Adrian Banks, Emrys Williams and Graham Stafford on guitars. Ann Taylor and Susan Roberts were vocals and Colin Gibson on drums. After Ann Taylor left in the summer of '67, Susan Lawton and I joined. This continued until the summer of '69. But John Worrell had left sometime before then. Ken Bridge was organising things in my last term there, and to be honest, the group was turning out to be more like a mini-choir, with the likes of Maureen Stubbs, Barbara Parry and Tina Parkinson joining. The original name was "Suzy and the Heartbeats" with Susan Roberts and David Grimshaw on vocals. From what I remember there was some argument between Susan Roberts and Ann Taylor about the group name till KB stepped in and said that rather than it be named after one person it would be better to come up with a collective name, hence the "Derby Diamonds!"' [E. Berrisford, FB, 2014]

It was in consultation with pupils that standards regarding the school meals were raised. The catering had been a major criticism for many years. Children's menus are adopted and both the quantity and quality of the food is improved. It was in this area that the impact of the new headmaster was first felt by all. Another early initiative by Ken was the introduction of television. John Blain remembers hearing the story of the struggle to get TV sets into the school. 'Apparently, most of the governors were dead against letting them in because they would be harmful to the pupils' already poor eyesight. KB challenged them to produce some credible evidence that a TV could damage eyesight and he would drop the idea.' No evidence was forthcoming, so under a rental agreement with Granada specially made TVs for education were introduced in all accommodation areas. These large 26-inch monochrome televisions, housed in wooden cabinets on tall metal stands, revolutionised the social lives of all [J. Blain, FB, 2014].

In 1967, Miss Ludden leaves and the next teacher to take charge of Class 2 is Miss Linda Williams. Another well-liked teacher who will remain long-term and play a major role in school life for many years to come with her love of the accordion and Scottish dancing, Linda boards at the school in the flat at the senior girls' end and when she is not teaching, dedicates much of her spare time to the children.

Gary Prescott arrives a year later and is one of a small group who spent his entire school life at Derby.

Gary Prescott 1968–1979

Gary was only five when he was sent to the school in 1968, spending just six months in mainstream education. Living relatively nearby in Wigan, Gary's parents could at least see him each weekend. At first, his father ferried him back and forth from school in the family car until by chance they discovered their local education authority had the allotted funds and the responsibility by law to provide this service.

After his parents made the necessary enquires, a taxi was provided to take all the children from the Wigan area home each weekend. Many children had their school experience dramatically improved by a half-heard titbit of information. How many more families could have benefited from additional visits from their children had other local education authorities come clean regarding their legal responsibilities?

Gary wasn't just lucky that he now had a taxi to take him home each weekend; his Uncle Jack was a travelling salesman. His job often took him past the school and when it did he would call in to see Gary and take him and a number of friends to play in the local park [G. Prescott, 2010].

For the first time in nearly twenty years the school expands. Accommodation within the hostel is found for the infants' playroom, creating space for a new seventh class. This new Class 2a becomes the remedial group and is taught by new teacher Jean Mills. Jean specialised in helping children who were behind with their reading and I fondly remember her teaching me using flashcards.

George Gooch remains up in the central block where his charges are now Class 3. This class also doubles in the evenings and at weekends as the intermediate boys' social area with the big TV at the back of the room. Ann Colbert's group becomes Class 4.

In 1969, Prince Charles is invested as the Prince of Wales and an estimated 500 million worldwide television audience watch live pictures of the lunar module Eagle land on the moon. The staff and pupils of Derby School are brought right back to Earth when the year ends in tragedy.

During the Christmas holidays, quite suddenly, Deputy Head Donald Taysum dies. He was the last of the original four teachers and his death is a massive loss to the school.

Returning in January 1970, Gary Prescott vividly remembers the announcement in morning assembly of the death of the Class 6 teacher. Gary was eight years old, and for him and many other youngsters this was quite a traumatic moment.

The school had recently added a new class and in light of the Education (Handicapped Children) Act 1970 a further revision of accommodation was needed. The Act pulled no punches. All children were to be educated. No child would be considered uneducable. There were thousands of children in training centres, special care units, hospitals and private homes. They were all to become the responsibility of local education authorities.

This Act encouraged even more children to be referred to special schools. New schools were opened, staff trained and the life experiences of thousands of "hidden" children were enhanced though education. Throughout the 1970s the movement to educate all children gathered momentum. Special schools like Derby were thriving [An Introduction to Children with Special Educational Needs, Second Edition, M Alcott, 2002].

In this same year Prime Minister Harold Wilson, who had been in power for most of the last decade, lost out to Edward Heath's Tories, and in Preston the vacant post of deputy head is taken by Kenneth George Townsend from Penwortham.

Ken Townsend arrives at the school to take on the duties of deputy head and Class 6 teacher during a snow blizzard in

January and was shocked to see children camping out in such atrocious weather on the lawn in front of the classrooms. He later discovered they were training for the Duke of Edinburgh award scheme.

Ken Townsend and Ken Bridge were soon to develop a strong working relationship that greatly benefited the school. The two "Kens", headmaster and deputy, worked well together, moving the school forward.

On the conduct of the children, the new deputy observed that the youngsters seemed to adapt to life away from home better than those who had reached their teenage years before being parted from their families [R.G. Crawshaw, 2005].

The school had a strict uniform policy overseen by Matron. Boys wore black shoes, short black trousers for intermediate and junior boys and long trousers for the seniors, white shirt with a red tie, grey pullover and brown checked tweed jacket. Girls wore the equivalent with a green tartan skirt. Children would also wear a second, "best" uniform on Sundays for church and other special occasions. This would include best black shoes, a green tweed jacket and dark green tie. Later, a yellow tie replaced the green and the green replaced the red worn for school days. In summer, girls had a complete change and wore a thin yellow cotton short sleeved dress, while for boys, concession to the heat was taking off their pullovers, but only after receiving permission. A boy could even get a "telling-off" for rolling his shirt sleeves up.

It was hoped parents would pay for their children's clothes, including uniform. On referral to Derby School each family was sent a list of essentials including uniform, play clothes, underwear, socks, comb, toothpaste, toothbrush and other necessities which they were expected to purchase. In practice, the school often replaced clothes from the stockroom. Some parents would find it difficult to keep up the expense and those of children who boarded all term would not necessarily be aware of their child's requirements.

The school's effort to create a "uniformed" look for its pupils wasn't restricted to clothing. Contrary to the fashion of the time, boys had their hair regularly cut short by two visiting local barbers. Glam rock was all the rage and the trend for boys was shoulder-length hair like the pop stars on telly, so the arrival of the barbers caused much unrest and protestation. Boys would be hard to find or suddenly become ill. On the other hand, there was no restriction on hair styles for girls. However, teachers were keen that a girl's fringe didn't fall in front of their eyes. Kathleen Owen (1969–1973) In "Keeping In Touch", 1995, remembers being embarrassed when Ken Townsend tied back her fringe in front of the whole class.

The medical welfare of the children was taken very seriously by the school, to such an extent that some disliked reporting an illness because of all the attention it created. The hostel had a medical surgery, a room by the far side (Black Bull Lane) entrance. Here, pupils would be administered before school with any daily medication, like Solprin or linctus from Matron or Ruth Collins. It was also the place to report any illness or injury. Up the nearby stairs and part of the juniors' dormitory area was the sick bay. Any child with an illness that required bed rest and quiet was isolated in this room. With the majority of the care staff stationed at the hostel, there would always be someone nearby.

Once a year a GP would visit the school and every child had an annual full physical examination. The doctor would be based in the surgery and children, when called, in groups of class and gender, would report up to the juniors' dormitory, strip off to their underwear and then one at a time come downstairs to the surgery for inspection. This whole operation was very embarrassing, particularly for boys, because the doctor was a woman. Sometimes, a child was required to be taken by Matron or another member of staff to the doctors', dentist or Preston Royal Infirmary (PRI).

Garry Cheesbrough
1970-1977

A few months before I started at the school, a visit was arranged for my family so we could have a taste of what was in store. I remember my dad pulling up outside the police station in Preston town centre and asking for directions to the school.

We were met in the hostel and shown round by Ruth Collins. Our initial reaction at seeing the school was one of great disappointment. It appeared to be everything a parent feared for their child: a dark, old Victorian institution. A few weeks earlier we had visited Exhall Grange in Coventry, a bright modern flagship school, and the contrast couldn't have been greater. The headmaster's improvements had hardly begun and the good intentions of staff were not clear for visitors to see. My parents had real reservations about me attending such a place, but in those days people tended to go with the opinions of so-called "experts".

A few weeks later I arrived at the school from Castleford, Yorkshire, in the local authority's minibus just before midday, on Monday 6th April 1970, aged nine years old. I was completely overwhelmed by the amount of rules, regulations and traditions of this strange little school. Nothing previously prepared me for the experience of boarding school life. I was put in Class 3, my form teacher George Gooch. At this time, the classroom was downstairs in the new block and doubled in the evening as the intermediate boys' dayroom. It felt strange to return to my classroom after tea to watch TV, draw, play and later have supper. I sat at my desk in pyjamas and dressing gown while Mrs Walmsley, the childcare assistant, gave out milk and biscuits.

That first day was very confusing. I subsequently discovered Mr Bridge had called a fire-drill practice; that and all the other bell-ringing, standing in line and marching here, there and everywhere completely disorientated me; for the first week I didn't know if I was coming or going. I got into a lot of trouble simply because I couldn't remember all the rules. There seemed to be an excessive amount of control which I just wasn't used to.

For Ken Bridge to sound a fire-drill on the first day of term was absolutely typical. He believed in keeping everyone on their toes regarding the dangers of a fire and regularly rang the alarm bell at the most inappropriate times. It wasn't uncommon to be woken in the middle of the night to the sound of the fire alarm and be marched down the drive to the classrooms for a headcount.

The school had a system of grouping children by ability before age, so although the youngest would invariably be in Class 1 and the oldest Class 6, this was not a set rule. Children didn't "move up" automatically by age like in mainstream schools. The school held half-yearly exams in January and July, and dependent on performance a child would remain in their class another six months or make progress to the next. It was not uncommon for a child to be younger than another in a lower class. A child's school report would detail how well they had performed against the other members of their class, while also stating the age range of the class. These two factors had to be considered together; a child could have an average exam result but be the youngest by a year or more in that group. I was labelled "below average" on arrival and remained in Class 3 for two and a half years.

The class teacher would undertake the teaching of all subjects, including games. The school had no specialist subject teachers. After the girls had left for their own lesson – cooking or needlework – boys would change for PE in the classroom. The PE kit was kept in a drawstring bag hung over the backs of the chairs: a bright red T-shirt, grey baggy shorts and plimsolls.

Kathleen Davies (née Owen) 1969–1973

Another child who found their first day rather traumatic was Kathleen Owen. She started in 1969 and never forgave the school or the housemistress for watching her take a bath. It was standard practice for the school to make every child take a bath straight away on returning, probably in an attempt to control disease, but it felt like an insult, insinuating we weren't being kept clean at home and being seen naked by strangers was something all new children had to learn to accept.

She went on to say she enjoyed the Christmas shows: 'I played the piano once and danced with Ann Colbert's dance group – "Ann's People".' (This was a corruption of "Pan's People", the dancers who regularly appeared on *Top of the Pops* at this time.) She added that of her time at Derby School, 'It was a time of caring in which to build confidence for life' [Keeping In Touch, 1, 1995].

With Ken Bridge the school developed a culture of pastoral care towards its charges. Out-of-class activities that help promote "character" like long weekend hikes or performing in music concerts, and shows that encourage confidence and self-esteem are felt equal in importance to traditional academic lessons. This policy, it was hoped, would help counterbalance any self-doubt a child may feel, having been labelled by society as disabled. The objective was for every child to attain his or her full potential, both socially and educationally, and central to that strategy was the annual Christmas show.

These shows were a perfect example of Ken Bridge's philosophy regarding the benefits of out-of-class activities. These productions spearheaded the strategy for instilling confidence and self-belief in the pupils, and as many children as possible were encouraged to take part. All schools attempt to nurture self-assurance and confidence in their students, but at a special school for children with a disability this was seen as a major priority. Practice and rehearsals were given high importance, equal to class work and therefore became a major part of school life.

A major component of Ken Bridge's unwritten "contract" for generating additional funds from the business community and his friends at the Rotary Club was the school maintaining an excellent reputation. It was essential that the school cultivate a good, positive friendship with the local community to facilitate cooperation with fundraising activities, and the Christmas show was the main thrust of that good-will strategy.

The 1970 Christmas show is the first without Donald Taysum at the helm. All the teaching staff pull together to take collective responsibility, each in charge of their own particular sketch or "number". The show opens with "Aquarius/ Let the Sunshine In" from the current hit musical *Hair*.

In the past, the show had been a typical pantomime or musical production, the kind most schools still perform today, but by 1970 this format is abandoned in favour of a "variety show" style performance. A succession of "acts", dancing, singing, sketches, short monologues and plays, held

together by a compere, telling jokes and introducing each act. This format enabled more children to take part.

The organisation and presentation of the shows were one great team effort by the whole school, and it was easy to be caught up in the excitement, fun and camaraderie of it all. Brain Machen says he was in four or five shows and remembers Ronnie Mileham had to be a steam train; he laughed so much he forgot his lines! Caron Ledger remembers being very nervous before "going on" and playing her accordion and dancing the "Charleston" and Susan Davies liked Miss Shepherd's items and thought the whole atmosphere was great [Keeping In Touch, 4, 1997].

Although the format was very flexible, there were a few regular numbers that popped up each year; the "opening number" would always be a loud and cheerful performance by the school choir under the tutelage of Mrs Mintoft, and "Ann's People" was four of the senior girls dancing to a popular chart record, choreographed by Ann Colbert. A Scottish dance number under the guidance of Linda Williams would find its way onto the programme along with a performance by the little ones in Miss Shepherd's class. Ann Hilton or Ken Townsend would oversee a short comedy play and Ken Bridge liked the old song and dance routine. The show would always end with everyone crowding onto the small stage for a grand finale. To help the cast find their position, the stage floor was painted with thick white lines.

On Friday, Saturday and Monday evenings across the last weekend before the Christmas break the show would be performed on one of the smallest stages imaginable. Parents, friends and family would squeeze into the tiny school gym over three nights to proudly watch their offspring, many travelling great distances to support their children.

For those three nights the school was turned upside down as it played host to a multitude of visitors. There was a ban on children going home that weekend so the school was really buzzing. The playground became a car park, the classrooms became dressing rooms and make-up room, and the laundry, behind the stage, became a bustle of frenzied backstage activity. Of course the gym and stage were given a Christmas makeover and as if space wasn't tight already, to the right, by the piano and under the Christmas tree, George Gooch based all his sound and lighting equipment.

Although Friday and Saturday were popular nights with parents, the Monday evening performance was the night special guests arrived. The school always managed to gather an impressive crowd of local dignitaries including members of parliament and mayors. The young performers would often take it in turn to look through the gap in the curtain at the "Chain Gang". At one Monday performance there

were six mayors and mayoresses, all with gleaming chains of office [Keeping In Touch, 2, 1996].

"Keeping In Touch" ex-Derby School pupils and

staff: 'Do you remember the Christmas shows...? Mr Bridge was our first victim for a *This Is Your Life*, and Ronnie Mileham was Michael Aspel. In his make-believe story Mr Bridge was supposed to have crashed, or was shipwrecked, during the war, on the island of Bora Bora. (Wherever that is!) The chief of the island gave him his only daughter in marriage. Raymond Thompson was going to be the daughter, dressed in a grass skirt. Unfortunately, he decided to develop appendicitis the day before the show and Mrs Colbert stepped in to fill his place. That grass skirt looked far better on her than on Raymond!'

The school built a good working relationship with Whittingham Mental Hospital, allowing pupils to gain valuable work experience there and taking the Christmas show on tour entertaining the patients. The hospital stage was vast, at least ten times larger than the small stage in the gym and possible to walk underneath from one side to the other.

One sound at the Christmas show that will never be forgotten was the laughter of a member of the childcare team called Mary Neary. It was so distinctive it was guaranteed to get everyone else laughing as well [Keeping In Touch, 2, 1996].

1971 is the year the problem with the intermediate boys' accommodation is finally resolved; Class 3 can no longer continue to double as a social area. To give the boys their own dayroom, a prefabricated classroom is purchased and erected at the top of the steps at the end of the original row of classrooms, near the boiler room. After a classroom reshuffle, this new class becomes Ann Colbert's Class 4 and George Gooch moves into her vacated room. He is delighted to now have his own class and no longer find spilt milk and biscuit crumbs on his desk each morning.

Miss Shepherd's Class 1 moves next door to the old Class 3 and is given some much-needed help supervising the very youngest when Jean Tomlinson arrives as classroom support worker. The large room that was once Class 1 is now the intermediates' day room.

Accommodation for the children remained like this throughout the remainder of the school's life. Junior boys and girls were housed in the Roper Hostel. Intermediate boys in the middle block, the newest part of the school and the senior boys and girls resided at the top of the hill in each end of the original main building. Children would mix in class time but were kept apart on all other occasions. Each had their designated social and play areas. The juniors was the only section where boys and girls could mix socially. Downstairs at the hostel they had their own play and TV rooms. They also had the gardens in front of the building.

Boarding accommodation and care staff

Girls	Boys
Roper Hostel Matron, Ruth Thornhill (Collins) Junior Girls 5–9 years old	**Roper Hostel** Matron, Ruth Thornhill (Collins) Junior Boys 5–9 years old
West Wing of original Elementary school building (Girls' End) Miss Jenkins/ Mrs Clarkson Senior Girls 9–16 years old	**New Middle Block** John Partridge / Leslie Thornhill / Graham Crawshaw (at different times) Mrs Walmsley / Miss Walsh Intermediate Boys 9–13 years old
	East Wing of original elementary school building (Boys' End) Frank Fairclough / Leslie Thornhill (at different times) Senior Boys 13–16 years old

The intermediate boys' dayroom was large and spacious, consisting of a pool table, television, lots of games and plenty of social seating, and they shared the playground with the senior boys. The older boys had a TV room, table tennis room and snooker room with books and a radio. In assembly girls and boys would line up separately and at meal times each had their own tables in the dining room.

The parent visiting days and school trips ceased. The last annual trip was to Knowsley Safari Park, near Liverpool, in 1971. Persistent rain meant the day was a complete washout and the children never left their seats in the coaches; it was felt the money could be better spent. With the rising affordability of car ownership and better public transport, most children had access to day trips and holidays with their families.

Three members of the teaching staff lived at the school and part of their job was taking responsibility for childcare after traditional school hours. They would take their turn at being "on duty" helping out the childcare attendants. George Gooch (Class 3) had an apartment at the senior boys' end of the main building and Linda Williams (Class 2) resided at the opposite wing, the girls' end. Ken Bridge occupied the flat in the middle of the building near to the intermediate boys' new block.

Out of these three teachers, one was more energetic in supporting extracurricular activities than any other, and that was George Lambert Gooch. At weekends, he regularly took groups of boys to the seaside in his Humber Sceptre and would organise Saturday morning football matches down on the field and a dance in the gym in the evening.

Beneath the main elementary school building were three cellars: two at either end of each wing and one underneath the centre of the building, accessed from outside by stone steps descending from the top of the main driveway, near a narrow or "coffin" door that led inside. George Gooch organised the intermediate boys to clear out and tidy up this cellar and then use it for hobbies and recreational activities, but the "Centre Cellar Club" hadn't been running long before it was closed down due to health and safety issues. There was only the one way in or out, making it extremely dangerous in the event of a fire.

The school's music teacher, Sheila Mintoft, visited each Tuesday to instruct the choir and take each class for music lessons and singing practice. This was the only specialist subject teacher the school had at this time. All day she would be based at the piano, right of the stage in the gym. Choir practice would be first, straight after morning assembly, and then each class would take it in turns to have a half-hour session. All things musical would happen on Tuesdays while she was available.

Sheila Mintoft would lead any choir performances, music concerts and play the piano during the Christmas shows. The school really enjoyed her sessions because she utilised a fair amount of modern popular music from the big musicals of the day like *Oliver!* and *West Side Story*. Not all made the choir, and those that didn't had alternative lessons, such as musical appreciation.

The school's "House" system was amended. A child would find themselves in one of three house teams with a housemaster. The saints of yesteryear were replaced with the names of the three main northerly rivers: Humber (yellow),

George Gooch; Mersey (blue), Ann Colbert; and Ribble (red), Freda Shepherd. Selection seemed to be random. The credit mark system was abolished; a way of rewarding good behaviour and class work with prizes creating competition, the main source of inter-house rivalry now was sport.

Sports Day was held each summer term down on the playing field. Children selected the events they wished to participate in and elimination heats were run in the evenings in the run-up to the big day. The event was run very similar to Graham's time except there was no prize money. Dependent on the finishing position, children would be awarded points and these would go towards their house. The team with the highest overall score would be the day's winners. Parents were invited, but, scheduled for a Wednesday afternoon, the day was always poorly attended as it required time off work and only local families would risk the weather being fine. If the day was ever spoilt by rain, plan B was to hold a singing concert in the gym. George Gooch could play the piano if ever it was required when Sheila Mintoft wasn't available.

One event always well attended was Open Day. This event was held in July near the end of term and unlike Sports Day, was on a Saturday to accommodate parents travelling long distances and encourage high attendance. Children who went home at the weekend would return for the afternoon with their families, and for those who boarded all term it was a real treat to see their parents at school. It was an opportunity to speak with the teachers, discuss progress and tour the school, discovering a little about their child's school life. Parents were introduced to staff and friends, in addition to being shown their accommodation area and dormitory, a valuable insight into the young person's life at

Derby School. But it didn't always go smoothly: 'I was very ill one Open Day and nobody bothered to tell my parents. My mum and dad couldn't find me because nobody told them I was upstairs in bed. My dad had an argument with Matron. He told her they were taking me home and she said he couldn't! I went home and stayed off school a week!' [Susan Elizabeth Kendrick (Davis), FB, 2014].

Not to miss out on the opportunity that all these visitors presented for raising funds, the school would hold a jumble sale in the gym and intermediates' dayroom. The stalls were run by the childcare staff and consisted of all the usual: white elephant, tombola and bric-a-brac. Prizes were donated for a grand raffle drawn by Ken Bridge in the gym at the end of the afternoon.

But for all these special days and events in the school calendar there was none more exciting and important to the children than "Going Home Day", particularly for those who hadn't been able to visit home at weekends. The term could be anything from five to nine weeks in duration and this felt a terribly long time to be away from the familiarity of home and family. Counting down to the last day of term with mounting anticipation was a major pastime and excitement grew as the last week approached.

On the surface, the last week would be like any other, but for the children this was a time of great joy and happiness. The first sign that this week was different came on Tuesday evening when suitcases were unlocked from storage and distributed so packing could begin. Once cases were open on beds, thoughts could really turn to going home.

On Thursday, the evening before going home day, with suitcases packed, the school would stage an end of term dance in the gym, a last chance for the pupils to mingle and socialise in their best and most fashionable clothes before parting for the holidays. This was a very enjoyable and emotional time; children knew all school work was over and it was time to party! The senior boys and girls made the most of their time together, knowing they wouldn't see each other for a week or more.

I remember in the intermediate boys' dormitory the night before going home day; none of us could sleep, we were so worked up. I used to wake about an hour early; lying in bed I could hear the quiet chatter and whispering voices of others. We were under orders not to get out of bed before the proper time, but there was no staff about to stop us. When the care assistants eventually arrived we jumped back in bed and pulled the covers up to hide the fact we were already fully dressed!

John Robinson leaves and his post of teaching Class 5 is taken by Mrs Anne Hilton. She became a firm favourite amongst the children, often staying back in the evenings, organising after school activities. Many children will fondly remember her bingo sessions in Class 1 on a Friday evening.

At a ceremony at the Odeon cinema, Church Street, Preston, with all the children invited, the school is presented with a "Sunshine Coach" from the Variety Club of Great Britain, in reality a white Ford transit minibus. This was an invaluable resource which had a major impact on weekend activities. Children could now be transported in groups. Rather than walking round the nearby area of Fulwood and Preston, hikes and camping in the countryside could be arranged for those remaining at school during the weekends. Trips each Friday afternoon to Saul Street Baths in Preston began, getting all pupils swimming, and Ken Bridge handed out "Breadth" and "Length" certificates in morning assembly.

A caravan is donated by the family of Thomas Howard, a pupil at the school, and installed on a site at Gisburn near Clitheroe. With the acquisition of the minibus, going to the caravan for the weekend became a regular occurrence. I suspect that the choice of site was more to do with the school getting a favourable deal than the attraction of the location. It was great for anyone who appreciates the roar beauty of the Pennines or who wishes to surround themselves by the landscape from the classic novel by Robert Neill, *Mist over Pendle*, but for us children it was just very boring. The only pastime available was walking the two or three miles along Burnley Road from the Todber campsite to the village, visiting the newsagent or sweetshop, playing in the park and then walking back along the country lane. When I first heard the school had acquired a caravan I imagined weekends at

1971		
Class	**Teacher**	**Approx. age**
Class 1	Freda Shepherd (Classroom Assistant Jean Tomlinson)	5–7
Class 2	Linda Williams	7–9
Class 2A	Jean Mills	7–9
Class 3	George Gooch	9–11
Class 4	Ann Colbert	11–12
Class 5	Anne Hilton	12–14
Class 6	Ken Townsend (Deputy Head)	14–16

Blackpool or somewhere by the sea; how wrong I was.

The routine was still very similar to that of the 1950s. Woken at 7.30am, lessons began after breakfast and morning assembly at 9am. A mid-morning fifteen-minute break and then two hours for dinner at 12 noon, one for the meal and an additional social hour before lessons resumed at 2pm. A mid-afternoon break and lessons ended at 4pm. In the evenings, "prep" and the activity hour were replaced with homework. All children from Class 4 upward had homework in their respective classes for an hour on Monday and Thursday evenings. On Tuesday, Ken Townsend held a remedial reading group in his class till 5.30pm for children identified as being behind their "reading age".

For the School Day	
Time	**Activity**
7.30 – 8.00	Woken up. Wash and dress. Pull bed sheets back to "air" bed. Line up and walk to hostel dining room for breakfast. Stand behind chair. Say grace and sit down.
8.00 – 8.35	Breakfast.
8.35 – 8.50	Leave dining room and return to dormitory to make bed and brush teeth. (Friday, change bed sheets). Wait for inspection. Line up and walk to playground.
8.50 – 8.55	Line up in playground in class order by gym door. File into gym, each class creating a line across the gym/hall.
8.55 – 9.10	Assembly. Mr Bridge addresses the school. Sing one hymn and say the Lord's Prayer. One member from each class walks forward to receive the post from Mr Bridge.
9.10 – 10.30	Children file out of the hall, in class order. Routine and begin morning lessons.
10.30 – 10.45	Morning break. Pupils either go to playground or the dayroom of their accommodation department. No one allowed in gym/hall.

10.45 – 11.55	Morning lessons continue to dinner time.
11.55 – 12.05	Return to each accommodation department, wash hands and line up for inspection. Walk down to dining room for dinner. Stand behind chair, say grace and sit down.
12.05 – 12.50	Dinner
12.50 – 2.00	Dinner break. Pupils either go to playground or the dayroom of their accommodation department. Not the hall. Some pupils may have extracurricular activities in class.
2.00 – 2.45	Afternoon lessons till break.
2.45 – 3.00	Afternoon break.
3.00 – 3.55	Afternoon lessons continue till teatime.
3.55 – 4.05	End of normal school day. Return to each accommodation department, wash hands and line up for inspection. Walk down to dining room for tea. Stand behind chair, say grace and sit down.
4.05 – 4.50	Tea.
4.50 – 5.00	Leave dining room and go to dormitories. Change into evening wear, "play clothes".
5.00 – 6.00 5.00 – 5.30	Monday and Thursday, back to class for homework. Wednesday, C.S.E. art. Tuesday, remedial reading class.
6.00 – 7.30 intermedi-ate (8.00) senior	Free evening time.
7.30 – 9.00 intermedi-ate 8.00 – 9.30 senior	Shower or bath, ready for bed, supper and lights out (supper at each dept, not dining hall).

Friday evenings were kept free as most children went home. It was requested that pupils return to school Sunday evening rather than Monday morning to prevent any possibility of being late and missing lessons. Children going home at the weekend were allowed to change from school uniform into their "going home clothes" during Friday dinner time.

When I first started at Derby School it was tradition to hold a school dance in the gym on Friday afternoons between 3.30pm and 4pm, a hangover from earlier times when the school had been a blind home. Dancing helped develop a sense of spatial awareness and a method of controlled socialising of the sexes. Everyone together in the gym made it convenient for parents collecting their children, but in the 1970s the old ballroom records were not popular. Children began requesting their own records to be played; but before this genteel dance turned into a disco, Ken Bridge stopped the event and opted instead to cancel the Friday afternoon break, shorten dinner time and finish school at 3.30pm, allowing parents more flexibility when collecting their children.

Individual students who were old enough and identified as of mature nature and reasonable eyesight could gain their "privileges". After receiving consent from parents, they were allowed out of the school unsupervised. This meant they could travel home at weekends on their own and those that remained could organise their weekends with more freedom, visiting the town centre or travelling further afield, like a day trip to Blackpool. Children who regularly boarded throughout the term and had a friend who went home at weekends could travel to their home and stay as a guest, all parties agreeing and consent forms completed.

For those who remained at school during the weekend the time was almost as regimented as the rest of the week.

Concession was given in the form of an extra hour in bed each Saturday and Sunday. Saturday morning, children wore their own "play clothes" and after breakfast basically had the morning free. After dinner, the mail was handed out and it was expected that the children should go out for the afternoon. This was in the form of a supervised trip into Preston, or if you were lucky and had your "privileges" you could go anywhere your limited funds would allow. On the whole, Saturday was quite relaxed, but all that changed on Sunday.

Sunday mornings meant a visit to church. This operation was organised with military precision. Children were forced to wear best school uniform with best shoes polished to perfection, a fresh laundered handkerchief in the breast pocket of their jacket and collection money in hand. Then the children were lined up for inspection with no excuses for not looking their very best. The church our presence graced was very much dependent on the member of staff taking us, but it was usually a short walk to Fulwood Methodist or a bus journey to Preston's Central Methodist on Lune Street. We sometimes visited St Cuthbert's Catholic Church on Lytham Road.

Sunday afternoon, and we were expected to go out again. This would consist of a supervised walk in the Fulwood area. Popular destinations would be Fulwood Barracks and Boys Lane. The park was also visited on numerous occasions. Children would walk by the old cotton mill and canal to Haslam Park, in the opposite direction to Moor Park near Deepdale football ground and sometimes into Preston, by the River Ribble to Avenham Park.

These leisurely Sunday afternoon walks were later exchanged for the rigors of hiking in the Pennies and across

Beacon Fell when the elderly childcare supervisors retired. The acquisition of the minibus and younger, more energetic staff like Leslie Thornhill allowed choice and ambition.

After Sunday dinner we exchanged our uncomfortable best shoes for more uncomfortable ill-fitting hiking boots. At the time it felt like forced hard labour, but the philosophy was to give the children who didn't go home a change of surroundings, beyond the boundaries of the school walls and into open space and fresh air. Sunday evenings would be spent welcoming back friends returning to school after their visit home and listening to tales of their weekend adventures.

Once back at school during the week, it was still possible to communicate with family. Tuesday was letter writing day. In class, children would discuss topics to include in a letter home and then write it out in rough. After checking the spelling and grammar, it would then be written in best in a book with carbon paper underneath to keep a copy. It would be one child's duty to collect all the letters from each class and take them to the post box across the road.

It was telephone night for the girls on Tuesday evenings and Wednesday for the boys. In an alcove under the staircase that led to Ken Bridge's apartment and the intermediate boys' dormitories, there was a large, heavy, black, old-fashioned telephone. Two children would "man" the phone on Tuesday and Wednesday evenings between 6pm and 7.30pm. Parents could ring; one would take the name and the other would run to find the child. This could lead to some frantic searches, particularly for children not expecting a call. In summer, when everyone would be outside playing down on the field, parents would spend more money waiting for their child to be found than they ever did actually speaking to them. But those phone calls from home were vitally important as Kevin Worsley explains: 'The isolation one felt as soon as you came back into the school. The phone call was a godsend. I remember once speaking to Mum and Dad and saying I wanted to come home and explained in detail the reason why. Matron was standing in the main corridor and heard every word. No privacy even when making a call home. I learnt one lesson: keep your trap shut and only speak at home' [Kevin John Worsley, FB, 2014].

Collecting the post and answering the telephone were just two of the duties children were given on a rota basis to assist in the smooth running of the school. Each Thursday dinner time Mrs Crean, the school secretary, would pin up a new "work rota" which would allocate a certain duty to a child for the coming week. These jobs included "security", making sure all classroom doors were locked each night; and "chair duty", placing all the chairs on the tables in the dining room after breakfast so the cleaners could mop the floor.

One job was taking the plastic clothes basket down to the laundry at the back of the stage each night. Many found this a bit spooky because it meant walking thought the deserted, silent gym and round the back of the stage to the laundry in half-light. Darkened Victorian buildings can play havoc with a child's imagination and ghost stories were common. The one job everyone hoped to avoid was "washing-up" duty. This required two boys washing up all the supper things, and, once finished, left no time to socialise before lights out.

In 1972, Preston and the surrounding area are thrown wholeheartedly into celebrating the Preston Guild. Throughout the summer, the town goes wild with festivities, the like of which many have never seen before. A funfair and attractions in Moor Park and at Avenham Park, music concerts and shows are performed on a specially erected giant outdoor stage. The streets are filled with the noise and colour of carnivals and floats. The school fully supports the merriment and attempts to involve children in as many events as possible. Ken Bridge grants "privileges" to a group of older pupils, giving them the freedom to plan their own participation. Not wishing to miss out on another fundraising opportunity, the school production line swings into action, children produce mementos and souvenirs for sale to parents and visitors. The "PP" and Preston coat of arms are everywhere!

The needs of potential high fliers are increasingly recognised and external examinations are introduced into the school. Firstly, the Certificate in Secondary Education (CSE) and later, the General Certificate in Education (forerunner to the GCSE) are taken in a number of subjects. But even before that, individual pupils had gone up the road to Fulwood High School for tuition in maths alongside normally sighted pupils, and at the end of the year they had taken the same O level exam. Armed with such recognised examination success, the brightest pupils moved up to A levels when they moved on from Derby School, and some of them even took a degree [R.G. Crawshaw, 2005].

In an attempt to move more in line with mainstream and adopt the system of specialist subject teachers to better prepare for CSE exams, children begin to move

80

around school to be taught in different classes. Teachers keep their form responsibilities in addition to a specialist subject. George Gooch is now science teacher, Anne Hilton mathematics, Ann Colbert is the art and French teacher, running a CSE art class on Wednesday evenings in Class 4. Ken Townsend's specialist subject is English. New staff member Morris Oakley is appointed and his remit is PE and religious education.

For the first time the school now has a specialist physical education instructor. He dedicated much time to gymnastics and introduced a cross-country run around the school, but the boys enjoyed playing football on the field the most. Morris loved to tell the boys that rugby was "his game", but the school governors would never allow that. There was a strict policy of no activity that could result in any sharp knock to the head. It was feared this was a danger to eyesight. Boys could play football but were not allowed to head the ball.

Morris was very proactive in arranging football matches with other local schools, but we nearly always got beaten. The game would start fairly evenly until the opposition put their first high cross into our penalty area. As soon as they saw we couldn't head the ball clear, they continued to pepper our defence with high balls for the entire game. They headed in goals for fun and all we could do was stand and watch. We were far more successful playing 5-a-side on the new tarmac playground. In "Keeping In Touch", 1995, Steven Foster (1970–1979) remembers being in the school football team and actually winning a game!

The "troubles" in Northern Ireland are constantly in the news and in the background of all current affairs. The conflict was the result of discrimination against the Irish nationalist Catholic minority by the unionist Protestant majority and the question of Northern Ireland's status within the United Kingdom. The violence was characterised by the armed campaigns of Irish republican and Ulster loyalist paramilitary groups. To begin with, the conflict was restricted to Northern Ireland only, but the IRA brought their bombing campaign to mainland Britain and anywhere could be a potential target [http://en.wikipedia.org/wiki/The_Troubles]. Bomb scares are common and the situation is made worse by malicious individuals taking advantage of the panic to raise false alarms, making hoax calls. One night, Derby School is the victim. 'The fire alarm was sounded in the middle of the night and we were evacuated outside to the yard in front of the blind workshops for about ten minutes and then told to go back to bed. We were just about getting back to sleep when the alarms went off again and Mr Fairclough told us to get out as quickly as possible and go down to the classrooms. A couple had been unlocked and after a short time we were joined by the intermediate boys and the senior girls, all just in our night clothes. It was about an hour before we got the "All clear"' [John Blain, FB, 2014].

To accommodate the more academically able, a policy of transferring the brighter pupils to Exhall Grange is introduced. Going off the results from annual internal exams, the top achievers are referred to the flagship state-of-the-art school in the Midlands. Not wanting to hold back the brighter children, they are persuaded to attend an institution that is acknowledged as having a greater array of facilities.

Founded in 1951 on the site of a former army base, Exhall Grange was located just outside Coventry in Warwickshire.

Like Derby, it was a boarding school for partially sighted children from across the country, but Exhall Grange had been purposely build for educating the visually impaired and incorporated many modern and innovative facilities, becoming a leader in its field. One such progressive idea was that all meals were taken in-house, as opposed to a central dining system. Many children lost friends who were "sent to Coventry" including, in 1973, my friend Kenneth Halshaw who took his O levels at Exhall. It became a family tradition because his brother Philip also followed him there.

It must have been very satisfying for those who had set them on the academic path. It was confirmation that the teaching methods developed at the school had created opportunities that were not there before, and it provided the evidence that had been lacking that at least some partially sighted children had abilities that had been previously untapped [R.G. Crawshaw, 2005].

Of course, the high fliers were by definition a small group and Derby School had to provide a stimulating education for all. That they did so can be judged from the number of parents who began to send their visually impaired offspring to the school by choice. Earlier generations of children had been "condemned" to spend their young lives at the school by ophthalmic surgeons who briskly completed the notorious BDN form but rarely took the trouble to visit. If they had done so in later years, these acknowledged experts could not have failed to be impressed by the performance of the children they had sent there, once they had been given the benefit of individual tuition at an appropriate pace. They may also have better understood the extent to which teachers had to develop an understanding of both the medical and the intellectual needs of each child [R.G. Crawshaw, 2005].

Under Ken Bridge's leadership, the school makes good progress forward, but many lingering old traditions still persist, as is only natural for an institution with such history; for example, the school calendar now permits half-term holidays and the length of term is, give or take the odd week, in sync with mainstream schools, but in the evenings Colin Brooks remembers childcare supervisor Mrs Walmsley who would constantly be heard asking 'Have you done your shoes?', referring to the obsession of making all children clean their shoes every night and take them for inspection [Keeping In Touch, 4, 1997]. Clearly, this links back to the boot making and shoe repair work of the blind workshops.

In 1973, the Partially Sighted Society (PSS) was created and registered as a charity. Founded from a parents group of partially sighted children attending Exhall Grange School and encouraged by headmaster George Marshall, the aim of the society is to support parents and children and offer an expanding range of services, catering for education, employment, social, domestic, and leisure needs for all. Recognising that only one in twenty-five registered "blind" people are without sight at all, the society makes no distinction between those registered "blind" or "partially sighted" [http://jim.leeder.users. What is PSS? 2011]. Recognising the positive contribution such parent-based groups could achieve, it wasn't long before "Friends of Derby School" was founded.

Graham Crawshaw joins the childcare staff as main housefather for the intermediate boys following the retirement of John Partridge. Graham had been a pupil at the school in the early 1950s and, constantly struggling to find lasting employment, thought he would turn to his old school. Graham brought to the school his

unique insight, having experienced life at the school as a young boy himself and with his love of photography. In the picture above are Graham and Mary Neary.

An internal telephone system is installed, greatly benefiting cross-school communications. In the past, if Matron in the hostel needed to speak with the senior boys' housemaster, she would have to walk all the way there or send a child with a message. Now they could talk by phone. John Blain remembers the phone system being installed: 'There was one right hand side of the stage not very secure, though. One day, when nobody was about, I had a play with it and found that if you gently pressed one of the buttons you could overhear the conversation for that extension' [J. Blain, FB, 2014]. The old phone under the central staircase is replaced with a modern pay phone, allowing children to make calls out for the first time.

Although the school was going from strength to strength, the country was heading for crisis, and our nation's problems couldn't be kept beyond the perimeter walls forever. To prevent rising inflation the government capped pay, including industry and the powerful mining union. By mid-1973, the NUM had encouraged their members to work to rule; this slowly led to a dwindling of coal stocks and the global oil crisis drove up prices.

To reduce electricity consumption and conserve coal, Prime Minister Edward Heath introduced the "three-day week" which began in January 1974. All commercial use of power was limited to three consecutive days. The working week became Monday to Wednesday. Schools were exempt from this ruling and able to continue, but businesses that supplied schools with goods and food were severely hampered. For some time there were food shortages, bread queues and rationing reminiscent of the war years.

In February, with support from the Liberals and Ulster Unionists, Harold Wilson returned to power for his third term. The normal working week was restored in March, but by October there was a second general election [http://en.wikipedia.org/wiki/Three-Day_Week, 2011].

The country was gripped by election fever, with two contests in one year, and catching the mood of the moment Derby School ran its own general election. Three pupils, each representing the main political parties, ran for office. They gave speeches and held rallies, culminating in a final debate on stage in front of the whole school. The Labour candidate won and when Labour's Preston North MP Ronald Atkins was told the result he visited the school.

It was important to teach the children typing. Proficiency in speedy touch typing was achievable with a visual impairment, particularly from dictation, and a good pathway to employment. The school had a few typewriters in a small room upstairs in the senior boys' end; this was cramped and inadequate. It was decided to requisition the boardroom, next to Class 1, which was only used about once a month (for the governors' meetings) and make this the new typing room. Big heavy Imperial typewriters were positioned on the green felt of the boardroom table, and for the new typing teacher, Mrs Booth, this became her base of operation.

After just one year in the job, Graham Crawshaw hands in his notice and returns to West Yorkshire. I think he found himself in conflict too often with other staff, his sympathy for the children and his enlightened approach not appreciated. He is replaced by Leslie Thornhill, from Sheffield, ex-army and a man who values the letter of the law, very different from Graham.

During this time, the school's programme of improvements is well under way. The facilities are continually improved. The lighting of once-dingy corridors is upgraded and carpets laid, the more spartan areas are glassed in and the central heating system greatly improved. Dormitories are painted in colours chosen by the children and lots of pictures are displayed, more toilets are added and showers introduced. The objective is to make the place more homely, and that includes replacing the old iron beds with wooden ones with drawer storage. Suddenly, there is room for possessions [R.G. Crawshaw, 2005].

Ken Bridge offered to replace the school's big, old black and white televisions with new colour sets. The senior boys preferred a stereo record player, so the intermediates got a new colour TV and the older boys received a top-of-the-range music system with diamond stylus. 'These were bought from the proceeds of a couple of mammoth "Jumble Sales" that were held in the gym. We went round the Fulwood neighbourhood to collect items from the local residents and raised several hundred pounds, which was quite an achievement back in the early '70s when you consider most items were sold for a few pence each. Anything of any value that was donated was taken to auction by George Gooch' [J. Blain, FB, 2014]. Many a happy evening was spent in the table tennis room listening to Elton John, David Bowie and a new band called Queen, while Frank Fairclough and later Leslie Thornhill battled to keep the volume down.

Soon after this, the school acquires a video recorder, a big Philips' machine, one of the first of its kind. It is connected to the intermediates' colour television and a number of pupils from Class 6 are instructed on its use to record educational programmes.

During the era of the Blind Homes and early history of the school, I have chronicled within these pages certain events that can only be described as "scandals" or at least examples of abuse of power or excessive control. No matter how well intentioned the vast majority of staff, there will inevitably be the rare outrage. One weekend, a houseparent responsible for the youngest in the hostel, angry after a relationship breakdown, adds cleaning fluid to the bedtime drinks, poisoning five children. They are rushed to hospital and spend a few days in intensive care. Concerned parents race to the Preston Royal Infirmary; those from far away are lodged at the school. Luckily, all the victims make a full recovery with no lasting after-effects. The perpetrator is dismissed and appears later at Preston Crown Court. In an age before any serious vetting of potential staff or criminal record checks, and little formal training for persons working with vulnerable children, it's a credit to the dedication of all that more "dark chapters" like this didn't occur.

Anne Hilton introduces a school banking system, run by the pupils to administer pocket money. Open during dinner time from Class 5, children queue up to make withdrawals and deposits. There are laws governing spending. Parents are told how much to give a child; this is 50p a week, and then that is controlled to prevent spending too much on sweets, and not forgetting 2p for the church collection box. Of course, most children could circumvent this system by receiving additional money at the weekend from home; it was the few who boarded all term that felt the full force of this strict fiscal policy.

The school's very last matron, Veronica Miroscoe, retires. Ruth Collins takes overall charge of childcare. She is happy to be referred to as "Miss Collins", having a far more approachable, less authoritarian style than her predecessor. Frank Fairclough retires and Leslie Thornhill moves from the intermediates to the senior boys to replace him.

1975: it's thirty years since the first school for the partially sighted opened and there are now twenty such schools throughout Britain, with approximately 2,500 pupils.

Class 6 responded to an invitation from the BBC current affairs programme for schools *Scene,* produced by Roger Tonge, asking schools to send in their own scripts. Derby School's proposal is selected and a nine-minute film entitled *We're Not Blind* is recorded after over nine hours of filming in and around the school. The show is originally intended to be a twenty-minute documentary, but because the school is a joint winner the presentation is divided into two nine-minute slots, with introduction and credits taking the remaining time.

It is an attempt by the children to put across to the public some of the problems and misunderstandings they encounter in the outside world.

Roger Tonge and his crew take a week to do the filming and add the "voice-overs". The whole of Class 6 visit the Manchester studios to see the rough cut. Later, three members of the class – Peter Dickinson, Kevin Worsley and Yvonne Green – travel by train to the BBC's London studios to comment on the final edition. It must have been a great experience for them all and a tremendous boost to the pupils' self-belief [R.G. Crawshaw, 2005].

This photograph is of Class 6 with teacher Ken Townsend, taken on the girls' lawn in front of the classrooms in the summer of 1975. Back row, from left to right, Garry Cheesbrough, David Powell, Glyn Jones, Geraint Fawkes, Kevin Worsley, Peter Dickinson, Paul Horsefield and Andrew McKiernan. On the front row, sitting down, Ferenc Schmidt, Janet Redfern, Kathleen Allison, Judith Adair, Yvonne Green, Erin Patterson and Terrance Kirby.

While the Blind Institute continued its business within the grounds of the school, the pupils' battle to distance

 themselves from the label "blind" was impossible. Ironically, the blind charity's presence actually increased with the opening of a new social centre, a prefabricated building by the senior boys' end.

There's quite a change around of teaching staff. Ann Colbert left six months earlier to have her first baby and now Anne Hilton joins her. Mr Hobday becomes the new Class 4 teacher, specialising in DIY and woodwork. Support assistant from Class 1 Jean Tomlinson takes over the responsibility of the CSE art class and new recruit Chris Philips steps into Class 5, mathematics teacher and head of the school bank.

1976 sees the second wedding involving school staff. The first had been in 1958 between teachers Donald Taysum and Evelyn Webb; this one, however, is two members of the childcare team. Ruth Collins, head of childcare, marries senior boys housemaster Leslie Thornhill. All the children at school that weekend attend the wedding and Paul Harrison, a senior boy, is best man. The ceremony is at the school's favourite church, Central Methodist on Lune Street in Preston town centre. The reception is held in the dining room of the Roper Hostel back at school. Together the Thornhills live and work at the school, taking the flat at the senior boys' end that was once Frank Fairclough's.

Jill Ryan (née Unsworth) 1973-1976

Jill was one of those children referred late to Derby School, already fourteen years old. She was at the Thornhills' wedding and remembers it well. She goes on to say she especially recalls Miss Jenkins, the housemistress, tackling an intruder in the girls' dormitory, always managing to sleep through the fire alarm and getting a right lecture from Ken Townsend for being kissed by one of the boys [Keeping In Touch, 2 & 4, 1996].

The policy of segregating boys and girls socially was strictly enforced and dates right back to the days of the Blind Homes when the Victorian authorities were outraged to discover that a blind man and woman wanted to get married! In the past, society had frowned upon relationships between disabled people because it was believed this would create more disabled children. But at this time the school is simply trying to dowse down any risk of a scandal. Relying heavily on donations and the good will of others, the reputation of Derby has a greater significance than a mainstream school.

Although George Gooch was a science teacher his resources were very limited. He'd filled his class with retro technology, old mechanical adding machines and typewriters, paid for from his own pocket, and although very popular with the children, they were more curios than learning resources.

To address a lack of science facilities the school joins forces with Lancaster and Morecombe College. Each Tuesday afternoon Class 6 boards the school minibus and drives up the M6 to study environmental science with tutor Mrs Jones. These sessions are great fun, many spent outdoors, involving field trips, visiting nature reserves and exploring the surrounding countryside and wildlife. In July 1976, Class 6 spent a week camping by Lake Coniston, part of their course. The highlight of the trip is walking along Hadrian's Wall. I remember really enjoying this visit and spending the summer holidays writing up a project about the Romans with plenty of drawings to illustrate the ancient wall.

The school often made partnerships with outside bodies to compensate for the facilities it lacked. The older girls regularly visited Glovers' Court in Preston town centre, availing themselves of the facilities to study domestic science while the boys played sports.

The list of evening activities is continually extended. In addition to those around from earlier times, the school adds archery on the lawn with Ken Townsend, badminton, cookery, Ken Bridge taught us how to make curry and do croquet, indoor hockey, volleyball, and Scottish dancing, with Linda Williams playing her accordion in the gym; all these in addition to the traditional Scout and Girl Guide packs.

One of Ken Bridge's pet projects is organising a Young Farmers quiz team. He is very keen to encourage the pupils to keep up with the news and have a good knowledge of current affairs, enthusiastically drilling the lads in preparation for competition. On Tuesday evenings the group would either host a visiting team in the senior boys' television room or play away. Ken would drive the boys to any away fixture, and if they won, which was quite frequently, he would treat the team to fish and chips on the way back to school.

Many of the children took part in the Duke of Edinburgh Award scheme, which provided a valuable boost to the pupils' self-reliance and physical fitness and developed a variety of skills including first aid, map reading and food preparation. The expedition required the same level of commitment as it demanded of participants with full eyesight, and it was not for the unprepared. The central task was a vigorous sixteen-mile hike over rugged terrain, followed by an overnight camp and a sixteen-mile trek back home.

For a school that had initially been reluctant to let its students out of the gates, the event was a major commitment – not least of which was the expense – every effort made to provide the hikers with the best in clothing, footwear, equipment and food. And there was the back-up too, with police, landowners and mountain rescue joining forces with staff from the school, in order to ensure that the experience was completed safely and satisfactorily. The success of the scheme could be measured in the number of bronze and silver awards, but the intangible benefits of achievement and growing confidence may have been of greater long-term benefit. Ken Townsend, who was a regular part of the support team, claimed to take his satisfaction from the mundane – there were no accidents and no one was lost on the hills [R.G. Crawshaw, 2005].

Ferenc Schmidt 1972–1977

One of the most popular pupils to attend Derby School in the 1970s was Ferenc Schmidt. Unfortunately, he was part of a very unlucky group of children for whom eyesight difficulties were really a minor problem in comparison to more serious health issues. Ferenc had cystic fibrosis (CF), which is a progressive lifelong condition in which the glands that produce mucus, sweat and intestinal secretions do not function properly. There is no cure, only supportive treatment [www.geneticdiseasefoundation.org, 2011].

Ferenc was clever and had a great sense of humour, as anyone who saw him perform the back end of a horse in the Christmas show will vouch. Stephen Foster 1970–79 best summed it up when he said, 'No matter how ill he was or how many tablets he had to take, he always kept cheerful and had a good word for everyone' [Keeping In Touch, 1, 1995].

1977 is the year of the Queen's Silver Jubilee and Virginia Wade wins the ladies' singles at Wimbledon. In May of this year, Ferenc and I, along with a few other classmates who have completed our CSE exams, are allowed to leave early at the spring bank half-term holiday.

I have changed greatly since arriving at the school in 1970. Back then I was a quiet, shy little boy who missed home, with a "below average" intelligence. I started in George Gooch's Class 3 and attended Jean Mill's remedial class and Ken Townsend's Tuesday evening book group to help catch up because my reading and writing was so far behind. By 1975 I am the youngest pupil in the top class, at thirteen years old, and by the time I have spent three years with Ken Townsend studying English and English Literature, my writing and spelling have vastly improved and I have become an avid reader. In seven years the school has completely turned me around. For the first few years my school reports always stated, "Garry needs to be encouraged to read more". By 1977, books are being confiscated as punishment because my head is always in one!

Throughout my time at Derby, my independence and confidence were encouraged and supported. I used to remain at the school all term, but by my last year I am travelling home by myself whenever I choose and during the weekends I remain, I take the bus to Blackpool. I feel I have gained a respectable well-rounded education superior to that of a mainstream school and decent exam results in seven subjects.

It was tradition for school leavers to gather in the headmaster's office for Ken Bridge to address us with a few parting words. He finished his speech by wishing us good luck for the future and then announcing we could depart any time that was convenient to us.

My local authority informed me that I was no longer their responsibility and I was left to finance my own journey home on public transport, another example of local council penny-pinching. It wasn't unreasonable to expect their responsibility not to end until I had arrived safely home, particularly when the minibus from West Yorkshire still arrived for the other children in my area and departed with empty seats.

The greatest criticism Graham Crawshaw had of the school during his time was the lack of preparation for the world of work. This deficit was dramatically improved during Ken Bridge's era. Apart from his great fundraising exploits, Ken will also be best remembered for his success in this area.

He applied both tireless effort and calculated logic to the task, researching the type of job he considered to be suitable and then lobbying the employers. He continually badgered his many contacts in the Rotary Club to take pupils who were most likely to give satisfaction – persuading Round Table members to give them mock interviews and a critical appraisal. Ken recognised that it would be a two-way process – a learning experience for both employer and employed – and he wanted each pupil to return with a reference stating that he or she had successfully completed a "normal" job [R.G. Crawshaw, 2005].

One of the prime benefits of work experience was the development of independence, and Ken insisted that all the participants should make their own way to and from the place of work. They were given the bus fare and required to make a packed lunch, but they were not allowed to accept a lift. The selected jobs were all considered to be suitable for a school leaver, with no special concessions made for defective eyesight. The work would be unpaid and everyone understood that it was the experience, not the remuneration that would be the reward. It was emphasised to the children that all of them would be volunteers; no one would be forced into work so that no one could say when something went wrong, "I didn't want to do this anyway." [R.G. Crawshaw, 2005]

The outcome was all that could have been wished for; eventually, there was only a handful of children that were never offered work experience and most returned after six or seven weeks with a prized reference. Several employers wrote to say that they would be happy to employ the pupils full-time, and occasionally a small sum of money would be given as a reward, but more commonly this would take the form of a small gift [R.G. Crawshaw, 2005].

A great help in supplying opportunities for work experience was Mr Michael Booth, director of Booths Supermarkets based in Preston, a great friend to the school and in 1977 made chairman of the Board of Management of the Blind Welfare. His ancestor E.H. Booth, the grocer, had been one of the original donors helping the blind institute get off the ground a hundred years earlier.

Michael Booth gave many school leavers job experience in his chain of shops in Preston and throughout Lancashire. Ferenc Schmidt worked for a time in the Poulton-Le-Fylde branch near his home and Tracy Ramshead went for her first work placement at Booths in Preston and is still working there today! [Keeping In Touch, 3, 1997]

Continuing in education was another option explored by the school. Pupils were encouraged to make contact with their local further education college, and groups of school leavers in their last year were taken by Ken Townsend in the minibus to visit RNIB (Royal National Institute for the Blind) colleges. This was taken up by some, but it meant another two years' boarding away from home so didn't suit all.

This situation was light years away from the culture that existed in the 1950s under Fred Rothwell when pupils were not even expected to graduate from school to the workplace and this, more than the harsh discipline and spartan lifestyle, was the greatest single failing of the school at that time but now, twenty years later, emphatically corrected [R.G. Crawshaw, 2005].

4

The Last Ten Years of the Derby School

1978–1988

By the time I left school in May 1977, Ken Bridge had been in charge for nearly twelve years and in that time he had truly achieved much, transforming his school from one that merely did a job and satisfied legal requirements to one that sought to excel. The school was small, with just over one hundred children, and any success would be relative to its size. In the years to come, the goal posts would be moved, bringing a whole set of new challenges.

All the time I was at the Derby School there were very few pupils from ethnic minorities. I knew of two albino Asian brothers and my good friend Albert Daley who was Afro-Caribbean. Albert's family had come over to Britain from Jamaica in the 1950s and settled in Telford, Shropshire. Albert was born and raised in England, but in my last year at school I experienced the phenomenon of at least two foreign pupils joining our ranks from overseas.

Partially sighted children were now being sent by their families from countries many thousands of miles away. Such was the growing reputation of a specialist education in Britain, parents would foot a very expensive bill to give their offspring the best possible chance in life, and Derby was one of those esteemed schools chosen.

The children sent were usually teenagers: mature enough to settle into a new school in a foreign country and able to stand on their own two feet for a few years while away living in Britain. This small group often found they were unable to return home during holidays and lodgings needed to be provided, sometimes staying on at school, but often the generosity of staff stepped in and they would be invited as guests to lodge with them.

Ironically, just as the population of the school was beginning to become more diverse and public opinion was shifting, with parents generally, at home and aboard, starting to appreciate the choice of a specialist school, the academic world was turning against such places. In the future, Derby School was going to need to diversify a great deal more to satisfy policymakers.

In December of 1977, Ferenc and I make a return visit to the school for that year's Christmas show. The only noticeable difference is that the senior boys now have a colour TV. It is satisfying to see others on the same progressive pathway. The young man compering the show began his time at Derby on the very same day as me. I went on to compere the show twice, in '74 and '75, and now here he is gaining that same valuable boost to confidence that only the buzz of a live audience can give.

With the publication of the Warnock Report in 1978, which advocated integration of pupils with "special needs" into mainstream schools, the future of specialist education was being debated in Parliament. Although the school was enjoying high attendance figures along with its foreign students and visitors from Australia, New Zealand, the United States and Yugoslavia who came and praised the work being done, the continued existence of such institutions was now open to question [R.G. Crawshaw, 2005].

Central to the ideology of teaching handicapped children before the Warnock Report was the belief that children in the company of others with similar problems would not be intimidated or bullied as in mainstream education, and therefore the atmosphere in class would be conducive to learning. Also, small class sizes, with the opportunity for more individual tuition, was thought very important.

But this philosophy labelled and segregated children, and boarding school life cushioned them from reality, making integration when they eventually left school to return to the real world difficult. This problem in part was due to the negative or naive reaction from the general public, caused by their lack of experience and prejudice when confronted with a disabled person. It was now felt integration was needed at a young age to help both sides.

While the arguments continued in London, the school carried on regardless. For about ten years now, Mrs Walmsley and Miss Walsh have been part of the childcare team working primarily with the intermediate boys. They are often seen together, but with contrasting styles, reminiscent of a comedy double act. Both middle-aged, Mrs Walmsley is tall and thin, a smoker and stern authoritarian. She keeps to the letter of the law; it is no joke to get on the wrong side of her, particularly when judging the polishing of shoes: something she had a very keen eye for. Miss Walsh was short, stout and very jolly, dedicated to the boys as if they were her own and always good for a laugh.

The stalwart of the senior girls is Miss Jenkins, who comes across as a bit of a battle-axe but is full of good intentions and very protective of her charges. Her lieutenant for many years is Mrs Clarkson and she is now joined by Mrs Finch. Another long-term carer is Mrs Brown.

The senior girls' end is a mirror image of the room configuration of the senior boys' department, but downstairs its use is different. There is a stock room for school uniform and a sewing room where evening supervisors can repair clothing. The population of girls at the school is only about thirty and this is split between two accommodation areas, the young at the hostel and the older girls at the seniors' end. There are no intermediate girls. Talking to ex-Derby schoolgirls, they felt overprotected and didn't feel they had the freedom the boys enjoyed. As the school attempts to limit fraternisation it is simply easier to have greater control over the smaller group.

The ground behind the classrooms neglected for so long is once again cultivated by the children under the supervision of Ken Townsend and transformed into a vegetable garden complete with greenhouse. His reclamation activities don't stop there. The senior boys find themselves waist-high in dirty water, clearing all the accumulated rubbish from Cadley Brook.

This is a "golden age" for the "special school" and particularly Derby School. Investment continues and the programme of improvements carries on as referrals hit peak numbers. Mr Bridge once told me that a local education authority paid more for a child to attend Derby School than it costs to send a student to Eton.

But with improved diagnostic techniques, allied with a greater understanding, more children are being found to have "special needs"; therefore a new approach is needed. It is now not acceptable, in educational circles, to refer to children as "handicapped" or "disabled".

All the metal-framed windows in the intermediate block are replaced with modern PVC and double-glazing. An additional fire escape is built at the foot of the dormitory stairs, giving access to the main driveway. A second prefabricated classroom is acquired and placed next to the existing one. This is named Class 4a and a young Mrs Walmsley, daughter-in-law to the childcare supervisor, is installed as art teacher. Next door, Mr Worsdale now teaches Class 4 and woodwork.

In a major move with significant investment, the school's partnership with Lancaster and Morecambe College ceases, and instead human biology is taught "in-house". Two of the blind workshops are requisitioned as operations retract, and the rooms vacated. For some time the school has used one for woodwork lessons, but now two more are utilised. The first class in the back of the institutes' workhouse with the entrance on the way down to the brook becomes Mrs Walmsley's art room. A second room is converted to a science laboratory and a new science teacher, Miss Julie Ann Wright from Mansfield, is appointed. The school had often been criticised for its lack of science facilities, but this has now been addressed.

The new prefab class that was Class 4a becomes Morris Oakley's base of operations and a percussion room. Children are taught drums and the vibraphone by Jack Wild, a specialist who visits each Thursday dinner time [P. Barnfather, FB, 2014].

When it came to upgrades the social areas weren't overlooked. The intermediates see their room transformed. In my day, I thought the room was large and spacious; now it is cluttered with a variety of leisure equipment acquired by donation. There are now two pool tables, table football, a pinball machine and a "Star Wars" video game in addition to an array of new shelving and furniture. Upstairs, showers are fitted in the intermediates' bathroom, one over each of the four baths. It was no longer necessary to trek down to the senior boys' end in dressing gown with towel and soap for a shower.

Evening activities are constantly revised and updated. The scout and guide packs are extended at both ends to accommodate cubs and venture scouts [R.G. Crawshaw, 2005]. The Young Farmers quiz team expanded to include a debating group. Peter Cleland was chairman of the Preston Disabled Speakers Group and talking in Galloway's Society for the Blind Newsletter in 2001 said, 'Derby School had a team who used to travel round to various venues. Nigel Walker, Vicky Swainbank and Reuben Parsons were some of the members of the team. Everyone had great admiration for the group who would speak confidently to over a hundred people in an audience.'

By 1978, school authorities are relaxing their attitude regarding freedom of movement in and out of the school, particularly when considering the nature of the establishment. Generally speaking, the older children probably have as much independence at school as they did at home, and in some cases, Ken Bridge may have given individuals more liberty than their parents would have allowed. This means that many of the local amenities nearby are regularly patronised by the residents: the newsagents down Plungington Road, the post office at Withy Trees and the local Spar. But the most frequented business by far is the corner shop right opposite the school.

Located on the corner of Plungington Road and Lytham Road, this little shop run by Mr and Mrs Sproats and featured in the *We're Not Blind* BBC documentary must have taken a great deal of business from the children over the years, supplying sweets, pop and crisps at dinner times, evenings and weekends. This shop would regularly be the first port of call before any outing or hike, everyone stocking up on provisions!

Another area of school policy that adopts a more liberal attitude is regarding the segregation of the sexes. During my time there had been a major effort to keep boys and girls apart at all times except in class, but now this has all changed. Probably prompted by the Sex Discrimination Act of 1975, both genders are now mixing at meal times and socially at evenings and weekends. The social areas of the senior boys and girls that once had strict limitations applied now have their borders dismantled, and for the first time these young people have full freedom of movement within the school as well as outside it. This new philosophy also applies to the curriculum; subjects are no longer divided for boys or girls. It is now the choice of the individual whether to partake of domestic science at Glover's Court or sport on a Wednesday afternoon.

Prompted by the new ideas coming out of London, teacher Chris Phillips embarks on a two-year sabbatical, investigating integrating visually impaired children into mainstream schools and working with the totally blind. Julie Wright is drafted in to cover his class [P. Barnfather, FB, 2014].

In 1979, there's a change of government; the Conservatives win a famous general election victory. For the first time, Britain had a woman Prime Minister, Margaret Thatcher. In Parliament the future of special schools is debated. Regardless of this, the school continually attempts to keep abreast of the times and utilise any new technology that can be purchased to assist the children.

The school widens its curriculum even further and begins teaching domestic science in the kitchens at the senior girls' end after many years of visiting Glovers' Court.

In 1980, Barbara Preston comes to the school as the new domestic science teacher. For a school that once had inadequate science provision, the children can now benefit from a timetable that includes human biology and domestic science. Paul Barnfather remembers: 'In human biology I always seemed to get partnered up with Linda Marsh for practical work like dissection of a heart. Julie Wright told Linda to take hers to Mrs Preston because she'd butchered it and it was only fit for a casserole! And my favourite of all was dissection of an eyeball as the last practical before I left. I was on a waiting list for a cornea transplant and Linda just stabbed right into the pig's eye and I ran out hurling my guts up' [P. Barnfather, FB, 2014].

Weekend camping trips and visits to the caravan at Gisburn continue during the summer months in the minibus. Ruth Thornhill now accompanies her husband, Leslie, along with the children on these expeditions which were really appreciated by those who boarded long term like Dawn Wilson; Maria Wharton remembers talking most of the night! [Keeping In Touch, 4, 1997] It wasn't long before the couple had an additional responsibility with the birth of their son, Duncan.

In 1980, the Thornhills are now a family and move to a new home in Fulwood. George Gooch, who has lodged in the flat at the senior boys' end for fifteen years, also moves to a house in nearby Much Hoole. This leaves no staff on night duty at the senior boys' end, so to plug this gap Ken Bridge relocates from his central flat to the old Thornhills' bedsit between the dormitories.

The flat vacated by George Gooch is unoccupied until Chris Phillips returns and uses the room to give additional support to a blind pupil heading to St Vincent's in Liverpool. [P. Barnfather, FB, 2014].

There is a reorganisation of classroom numbering. Ken Townsend's class is elevated to Class 8. It appears the woodwork and art and science rooms in the blind workhouse are not numbered; also without a number is the percussion room next to the now Class 5. The school has never been in such good shape, double the original number of classrooms and boasting other specialist facilities. In all classrooms a range of electronic aids are brought into use.

1980		
Class	**Teacher**	**Location**
Class 1	Jean Mills	First class in row
Class 2	Freda Shepherd (Classroom Assistant Jean Tomlinson)	Top of the driveway in the "new" block
Class 3	Linda Williams	Second class in row
Class 4	George Gooch	Third class in row after headmaster's office
Class 5	Mr Worsdale (Woodwork)	First prefab at top of stairs
Class 6	Mrs Walmsley (Art)	Fourth class in row next door to class 4
Class 7	Chris Phillips (Maths)	Science lab in blind workhouse
Class 8	Ken Townshead (Deputy Head)	Last class in row

CCSTV enables the enlargement of the printed word, and large calculators provide similar numerical help. Wooden chairs are replaced by modern plastic, but the characteristic old desks that hinge, bringing work up nearer to the eyes, remain [R.G. Crawshaw, 2005].

Julie Wright promotes science even further in the timetable. She pilots a CSE general science class on Wednesday evenings from 5pm to 8pm in her science lab. There are just four to six boys in this group who are also taught physics in the second year of this two-year course. These small class numbers must have been a great advantage to the learners.

The 1981 Education Act had major implications and marks the beginning of the end for the Derby School and many other special boarding schools, at least in their current form. Drawn up in the immediate aftermath of the Warnock Report, published in 1978, it is this Act which provides for disabled children's rights to integrated education as opposed to segregation. The Warnock Report, published by the Warnock Committee, entitled "special educational needs", put an end to labels previously used in education such as "handicap" and replaced them with "special educational needs" [R.G. Crawshaw, 2005].

In the wake of this Act, Margaret Thatcher set out on a major public relations exercise, visiting a number of special schools to demonstrate that she and her government personally had nothing against such institutions or their inmates. Derby School was probably too insignificant and northerly to take her interest, but she did famously visit Exhall Grange. This was covered on television, making the local and national news.

Also in 1981, Mary Neary, childcare worker, retires after twenty years' service working in the hostel and senior girls' end, but living so close to the school it's hard to keep her away! She continues to find numerous reasons to return and visit the children. One of the school's great characters and a genuinely loving, caring woman, the school loses a great servant, but she remains a good friend. The school probably employs about twenty or more childcare workers at any one time, nearly all part-time, working either in the evenings or mornings with just a small core full-time. Over the years they come and go and it is near impossible to name them all.

It would be some years still before the impact of new policy begins to bite. In the meantime, it was recognised that the school's needs were exceptional, as it sought to acquire any specific aid that the experts recommended for the children with visual difficulties, and outside the walls there was the continued march of progress that the school tried to match [R.G. Crawshaw, 2005].

The amazing potential of computers is immediately recognised while they are still in their infancy and introduced. The school has always understood the importance of keyboard skills and computers are a natural progression from typing practice. Julie Wright's science lab is equipped with BBC model B computers [P. Barnfather, FB, 2014].

An additional housefather is employed to help supervise the senior boys under Leslie Thornhill and lodges in the flat once home to George Gooch. After returning to school one evening drunk and threatening violence towards a number of boys he is instantly dismissed. During my research for this book I have found that Ken Bridge and the school governors are quick, decisive and professional when dealing with staff misconduct, but there was also a tendency to attempt to silence the children into not mentioning such incidents to their parents. With the school's reputation on the line, its clear Ken would be under extreme pressure, but this behaviour cannot be condoned, and anyway it would be near-impossible to stop children talking. Parents of the boys concerned found out and one mother arrived together with an education welfare officer. This official informs the school that his local authority will no longer refer children to Derby School [P. Barnfather, FB, 2014]. I suspect that the decision wasn't just because of this unsavoury episode but because many local councils were now questioning the wisdom of referring children to special schools.

The relentless drive for modernisation continues. In an atmosphere of uncertainty the Board of Management sustain their backing of Ken Bridge and his improvement programme. Finally, the classroom row is given the attention it has long needed. The classes are enclosed within a brick and double-glazed corridor. This walkway extends to the side of the hostel, enabling access from the dining room to Class 8 without having to brave the elements. The steps down to the classes are included in this build, partially obscuring the windows of the prefab class, resulting in them having to be filled in. The classroom ceilings are lowered and their windows replaced. Although this is a major improvement it sadly changes the character of the school and how many remember it forever.

The picture on the next page shows the school with its additional classrooms and covered walkway. This is how the school was to remain for the rest of its life.

In February 1982, after a long and debilitating illness, my school friend Ferenc Schmidt finally loses his battle with cystic fibrosis, a struggle he fought so courageously and with such spirit all his short life. He was just twenty-one years old. After leaving school Ferenc worked in the local branch of Booths Supermarket, his plans for college abandoned because of his illness. While in hospital he wrote an essay about his thoughts on life, of which I feel very lucky to have a copy.

The funeral service is held in his home village church in Poulton-Le-Fylde with family and many friends, staff and acquaintances from Derby School present. In fact, there are so many people who wish to attend the service that the church is overwhelmed and a large crowd follows the service from outside.

Chris Phillips leaves Derby for a post advising local education authorities how best to integrate visually impaired children into mainstream schools. Ironically, this work is contributing to the demise of the school. He is replaced by Miss Linda Brindle [P. Barnfather, FB, 2015].

Later that year in April, after an attempt to occupy and claim the Falkland Islands, hostilities break out between Britain and Argentina. Many see the victory of this South Atlantic conflict as helping Margaret Thatcher and the Tories back to power in the general election of 1983. This election win dashed anyone's hopes that a change of government may bring a change of policy regarding the closure of special schools. At this time

there are many who link Margaret Thatcher and the Tories with the policy of closing special schools, but the Warnock Report was drawn up during a Labour government and the logic of the argument crosses party politics.

The Christmas shows of the early '80s continue to be a major fixture in the school calendar, using the same tried and trusted format of old but with some technical advances. The 1983 presentation is themed "Thanks for the Memory". There are two microphones hanging from the stage ceiling to capture sound and the whole performance is videotaped in colour using a camera loaned from the BBC. This is significant for anyone, like me, interested in the school's history because from now on all major events are filmed.

The stage is extended by removing the footlights and front lip and placing tables in front, creating a step down but giving more room. The show is very reminiscent of the 1976 themed *The Good Old Days* and included the same famous musical number by Judy Garland from Easter Parade, "We're a Couple of Swells", this time performed by two different children for a whole new audience.

Joanne Morris played Barbara Woodhouse, the animal trainer, in one show, with someone dressed up as her dog. On the last night the dog did the opposite to what she told it. The audience really enjoyed this, but Joanne couldn't understand what was happening until she saw Mr Worsdale laughing in the wings. Tracy Ramshead remembers a sketch where two people were dressed up as a cow, also being in pyjamas with four others singing "Me and My Teddy Bear" [Keeping In Touch, 4, 1997].

Another year, the show became a circus and attempted to expand from the confines of the small stage to engulf the whole of the hall. Mrs Walmsley (art teacher), Mr Worsdale and others decorated the gym to look like a circus tent. Midway through the second half of the production a cannon was fired which propelled a dummy halfway down the hall [Keeping In Touch, 2, 1996].

In 1984, falling numbers of referrals are beginning to affect class sizes. The average number of pupils in any one class has always been around fourteen to fifteen, but now the photo of the class above shows just ten children.

However, the Derby School isn't the only place where

people anxiously contemplate job security and the closure of their place of work; this is the year of the miners' strike. The dispute starts when the government announces the closure of Cortonwood Colliery in Yorkshire. This was to be the first of twenty pit closures with the loss of 20,000 jobs. The NUM responds by calling for a national strike [strike84. co.uk, 2011]. Although this is a major industrial dispute, unlike in the 1970s, the school continues to operate almost unaffected.

Julie Wright marries, becoming Mrs Lewis, and after more than ten years of loyal service the caravan is brought from Gisburn to the school and set down on the playing field. There is a torrential downpour that floods the field and the caravan is destroyed. A sad end; many children will have fond memories of weekends spent at the caravan and the village of Gisburn, me included. For many years it was a welcome change of surroundings for those who didn't go home at weekends.

Although still susceptible to flooding because of its low level by Cadley Brook, the school playing field benefits from much hard work over the years. When the school first opened it was being used as grazing pasture by a local farmer; during my time there was just one main field cut and marked for games, while the first field was still hedged and overgrown. By the main field was overgrown banking leading up to the surrounding housing estate and there was embedded concrete from some past building. Now both fields and embankment are one. Hedgerows and concrete have been removed, leaving a large space nicely cut and maintained. The field is now a much improved and safer recreational environment.

In March 1985, the year-long miners' strike finally ends. It is a defining moment in British industrial relations and the defeat of the NUM significantly weakens the trade union movement. It was also seen as a major political and ideological victory for the Conservative Party and enabled the government to consolidate its "free market" programme.

In that same year, Freda Sheppard, teacher of the very youngest children, retires after twenty-eight years (1957–1985). She is the longest-serving teacher in the school's history. In her time she witnessed many changes. Arriving in the era of Fred Rothwell and Donald Taysum, when the school was just over ten years old, she will remember the children bringing their own magnifying glasses and large print books in short supply. She now leaves a school where the pupils have all the latest visual aids, a science classroom and access to computers. Jean Mills teams up with Jean Tomlinson to continue the work of teaching the very youngest.

During the summer holiday, Wembley Stadium stages the Live Aid concert for the starving in Africa, raising a global £30 million. Described as the Woodstock of the '80s, the world's biggest rock festival is organised by singer Bob Geldof to raise money for famine relief.

Maybe because of a dip in pupil numbers, there's a break with tradition and the usual format for the Christmas show is abandoned. For the 1985 presentation the stage is transformed and the audience transported to "Never Never Land", populated by pirates and Red Indians for the pantomime *Peter Pan*. This show boasts some of the best scenery and costumes of any performance. Highlights include four boys performing a Hawaiian serenade dressed

in coconut bras, grass skirts and sporting moustaches, surely inspired by Freddie Mercury, popular lead singer with rock band Queen. In keeping with pantomime tradition the cast attempt a little audience participation as they cajole the Chain Gang to sing along!

Unsettling times are just around the corner as rumours begin to circulate regarding the future of the school. The overwhelming opinion amongst parents and staff is opposition to the new government policy of integration, believing children would suffer without specialist schools. Care staff and teachers are also understandably anxious about their jobs and livelihood.

The school would not go down without a fight, and a campaign to keep operating was launched. Tactfully, all employees have to keep their distance so as not to appear self-interested. The fight had to be purely about the future direction of education for visually impaired children, their interests only. To this end a Parents' Action Group is formed and Eileen Birkett, mother of school pupil Anna Birkett, is chosen as spokesperson.

This campaign to champion special schools and keep Derby School open culminates in a well-publicised march on Downing Street in April 1986 and a meeting outside No. 10 with the Iron Lady herself, Prime Minister Margaret Thatcher. The Parents' Action Group together with a large group of children all travel down to London for the day. In perfect spring weather for an outdoor protest they hand over a petition of 16,000 signatures. The demonstrators crowd behind the Downing Street barrier carrying placards with slogans such as:

"Save Our School"
"Can't you see? Derby School is needed"

A very clever one exclaimed:

"Let us stay NORMAL in a special school NOT SPECIAL in a normal school"

This confrontation was covered by local television. Eileen Birkett, spokesperson for the action group, when speaking to a television reporter summed up the view of everyone present when speaking about the school. She said: 'It's the only one in the North that can cope with partially sighted children. We have wonderful caring staff, every facility imaginable for the children; the teachers are aware of their handicap and can cope with the children. To me, you put those children in a normal school and it's not integration; as far as we are concerned, it's segregation.'

Margaret Thatcher spoke to Eileen and the children for a short while, making a great effort to show she totally understood and sympathised with the situation, saying she knew all about their grievances but then made a right blunder live on camera when she assumed the children were from a mental institute!

The reporter went on to state that 'The 1981 Education Act doesn't specify that disabled children must be integrated into mainstream schools, but it should be the aim where able-bodied pupils will not suffer from the mix. Children and parents are convinced there is latitude within the Act for the best specialist schools to survive and they hope Mrs Thatcher, with her enthusiasm for freedom of choice, will now do her bit to keep Derby School open.'

The school did have an option that would have secured its future but involved changing the nature of the role it preformed. The Board of Management needed to make the decision to diversify. Although the 1981 Education Act wanted local authorities to fund educational provision for children with "special needs" within their local mainstream schools, there would always be some children with special needs, so demanding or requiring such specialist attention with a special educational statement at an "ordinary" school would still be wholly inadequate.

This category of child would still require the support of a specialist school, but numbers were so small, schools that chose this option would need to be geared to cater for multiple types of special educational needs. It would not be financially viable to focus on one group, for example visual impairment.

Exhall Grange was one of a number of special schools that took this new direction and is still open today, but it's completely unrecognisable from headmaster George

Marshall's time in the 1970s and early '80s. St Vincent's in Liverpool is another. This was very similar to Derby: a small school run by a blind welfare for partially sighted children. All pupils now have a statement of special educational needs. In recent years, the population of pupils has changed and many now have additional needs to their visual impairment. These include: communication disorders, autism spectrum disorder (ASD), cerebral palsy and hearing impairment [www.stvin.com, 2011].

Also appearing in this news report was Ken Townsend, shown teaching in his Class 8.

After just over twenty years' service, and conscious that while headmaster he couldn't get involved actively in this fight for the survival of the school, Ken Bridge makes a major decision. In May 1986, he decides to retire. He would hand over to Ken Townsend at the end of term. A committee was secretly formed, including Jean Mills and Ruth Thornhill, to organise a surprise retirement party, and donations were collected to purchase a leaving present.

A couple of months later at the beginning of Sports Day, Ken Bridge, a little disappointed at the small parent turnout, announces that it will be his last as headmaster. He goes on to explain that it's also the last for PE teacher Morris Oakley. At the end of term, Morris will reluctantly be taking voluntary redundancy as the school is forced to make cutbacks. Although tainted with sadness, it's business as usual for the present and it's a beautiful day, perfect for sport.

All pupils, teachers and care staff make their way over the bridge and down to the field carrying chairs and equipment. Parents take their seats and watch on as Ken

Townsend lines up the participants. Jean Mills officiates at the finishing line. The points are all calculated and Mr Oakley announces the results through his megaphone.

The children still compete in their "house" teams; now they have coloured team shirts, and the races and events are the tried and trusted formula of old. By the end of the afternoon Mersey are crowned winners and bottles of pop are handed out to all but not before the chairs are taken back up to the gym!

During the last week of term, in July 1986, the hall is decked out for a party. A special cake baked by Barbara Preston,

domestic science teacher, takes pride of place at the front by the stage. A senior boy acts as DJ, playing party music to a packed crowd of institute board members, staff and children as they welcome ex-staff and ex-pupils for a grand get-together to celebrate Ken Bridge's twenty-one years as headmaster of the Derby School and look back over his many achievements during that time.

Eventually, as the evening progresses, the formalities begin. Mr Michael Booth, chairman of the Board of Management of the Blind Welfare, takes to the front of the stage to make a speech. He described how he first met Ken at Woodville, covering him in mud as he helped push his car out of a field, and then how in 1965 he arrived and began the process of turning an "also-ran" school into "something out of this world".

Although the school is experiencing anxious times he tries to rally morale and is upbeat and optimistic in tone. He states that the management have plans to further develop the school. He ends by presenting Ken with a gift from the board in the form of a video recorder.

Ken Townsend then says a few words. He chronicles all the improvements made to the school over the years, emphasising the difference Ken Bridge made. He goes on to tell a funny story of the time Ken left his car keys in his flat in Preston and then locked himself out! All this on the night of a Christmas show; he was lucky a neighbour drove him to school, but he was a little late. I remember Mr Bridge often locked himself out of his office and he would take me out of lessons to climb through his office window and unlock the door from inside!

Then, to his great delight, the parting headmaster is presented with a computer to assist in his work as chairman of the education section of the Partially Sighted Society. The collection raised £1,495 and was used to pay for a holiday on the Orient Express! Finally, there is one last surprise as the curtains are drawn back to reveal teachers and childcare staff, accompanied by Sheila Mintoft on piano, singing "Thanks for the Memory" from the Christmas show of a few years ago.

It must be acknowledged that during his time Ken Bridge achieved much, but taking the school forward was only possible with the backing of the Blind Welfare Board of Management and the support of people like Chairman Michael Booth.

When school returns after the summer holiday in September 1986, Ken Townsend is in charge of just seventy registered children. No doubt he would have preferred to have taken over under happier circumstances. He inherits a situation of falling pupil numbers and a reduction in the associated income as local authorities change policy in line with new government thinking and stop referring children to the school. Mrs Clay, a local teacher wishing to gain experience of children with special needs, is drafted in as deputy head, English and Class 8 teacher [M. Riley, FB, 2015].

These last few years are quite chaotic, especially for record-keepers and people like me attempting to chronicle its history. Teachers are coming and going as long-term

employees are pensioned off to be replaced by others on short-term contracts, and all teachers are moved about as classes merge to help manage falling numbers. In just a very few years the school has gone from expansion and record numbers to retraction and rapidly falling referrals.

In June, the Tories win a third term in office, and at a meeting in August 1987 the inevitable is finally accepted that the battle is lost; it is decided the school will close.

When the very last term in the history of the Derby School starts in September 1987, welcomed back are just forty-six children [R. Alker L.E.P, 1987], and in the autumn the whole school go on a day trip to London to use up the remaining funds [M. Riley, FB, 2015].

The pupils and staff of the school have dwindled to such small numbers that they can all gather in the gym in front of the stage and appear all together in one photograph.

There are many long-term teachers still with the school during this very last term: Headmaster Ken Townsend, Jean Tomlinson, Linda Williams, Jean Mills, and George Gooch, and from childcare the ever-present Leslie and Ruth Thornhill. During this last term, children are found places in mainstream schools in their own neighbourhoods. The last pupils to leave are those taking their GCSE exams. Anthony Walsh left in May 1988 following appendicitis. He remembers sitting his English exam and then being taken to Preston Infirmary by Ruth Thornhill for his operation [A. Walsh, FB, 2014].

The trustees decide during the summer break to put the school buildings up for sale; they need to hand over the site immediately after the last pupils leave at the end of the summer term, July 1988. Once the decision has been made it is only financially prudent to hand over ownership as quickly as possible; the blind welfare doesn't want to be paying utility bills and rates for empty buildings that are not generating income.

The school closing makes the local newspapers, with headlines "Sale of Derby School ends historic chapter" and "Lights go out for blind school". It is very disappointing that even in 1987 journalists still can't make the distinction between blind and visually impaired. It seems that for some the school will always be a blind home.

The school and the seven-acre site, including the five-acre sports field, are made available to the highest bidder. Advertised locally and nationally by the commercial division of Black Horse Estate Agents, offers are sought in the region of £250,000. Excluded from the advertisement was the Roper Hostel, which is retained as a base for continuing welfare work for the blind and partially sighted of the area [R. Alker L.E.P, 1987].

The advertisement states that the buyer will be getting substantial Victorian buildings erected by public subscription, fundraising and bequests at the end of the last century. General Secretary of the Institute Eric Halstead said, 'We are bound to get the best possible price we can for the premises and the sale has to be approved by the Charity Commissioners. The money we get from the sale will be invested and used to expand our welfare work. We now have two social workers and would like to increase our outside work.'

The Education Reform Act of 1988, although now of no relevance to Derby School, is widely regarded as the most important single piece of education legislation in Britain since the "Butler" Education Act of 1944. Grant maintained schools (GMS) are introduced. Primary and secondary schools could, under this provision, remove themselves from their respective local education authorities and be completely funded by central government.

The national curriculum (NC) and "key stages" (KS) are introduced. At each key stage a number of educational objectives are to be achieved. An element of choice where parents can specify which school is their preferred choice is adopted and our obsession with league tables begins. It is this Act that introduces most of the familiar elements we find in our schools today [wikipedia.org/wiki/Education_Reform_Act_1988].

In July 1988, after fifty years as the Fulwood Blind Homes (1895–1945) and forty-three years as the School for the Partially Sighted and then the Derby School (1945–1988), the institution finally closes. The Blind Welfare has been established on the premises in Fulwood for ninety-three years.

The last remaining children are accepted into their local mainstream schools armed with statements of special educational needs come September. The Preston and North Lancashire Blind Welfare Society continues on, but they are forced to relocate all activity to Howick House in Penwortham, Preston. This is the Blind Welfare's second base, purchased in 1951.

One week after the end of term there is a final great Open Day Reunion. The following Friday afternoon, after all children have departed for home, gates are flung open and teachers, care staff and pupils, past and present, gather for a grand celebration of a once unique and very special little school.

During the preceding weeks, an extensive archive of contact details was utilised in an attempt to invite as many people as possible who have had some connection with the school throughout its long history, some returning just two years after last visiting for Ken Bridge's retirement party, and others making the pilgrimage after a great many years. This is a chance for old friends and acquaintances to meet and catch up with one another while making a last tour around the grounds and buildings before the property is handed over to its new owners.

Ken Townsend and Ken Bridge enthusiastically welcome visitors at the top of the drive by the French windows. The passing of the years has changed people and it's a struggle for some to recognise each other. These once schoolchildren are now adults and in some cases have children of their own. For example, I return to the school with my wife, Ann, and our baby daughter, Hayley. While my old teachers marvel at the fact I am now a father, I am surprised at the changes to the school. I never expected such extensive improvements. It's ironic and sad that the school is closing at a point in time when it's never been better equipped to continue.

From my point of view, I'm a little disappointed. I was hoping to visit my old school, but this doesn't feel like the same place where I spent seven years of my childhood. A number of friends I was hoping to see don't appear, either due to out-of-date contact details or having other commitments. But I also have to accept that for some of my old classmates Preston and the whole boarding school experience is difficult to reconcile. There will always be a number of ex-pupils who feel resentment or harbour grudges and have no wish to return.

With a group of friends we explore the school. The classrooms have changed the most. The gym with its little stage is very familiar and brings back memories of many happy evenings spent dancing with girlfriends and performing in shows and concerts. Work on clearing the intermediates' dormitories has already begun, wardrobes gone and bedding packed away: a very disappointing scene. But without a doubt, the highlight of the tour is visiting the senior girls' end and their dormitory for the very first time! I take childish delight in entering an area of the school that was strictly out of bounds during my time there.

Everyone makes their way down to the hostel, where the dining room becomes the centre of all activity. A large buffet is spread out and people queue at the hatch for tea or coffee and grab a bite to eat. The room is buzzing with excited chatter as everyone has a lot to discuss. For some, this is a very emotional time as important friendships are renewed and past experiences recalled.

During festivities a double presentation is made. A member of the Board of Management of the Blind Welfare apologies on behalf of Chairman Michael Booth; he explains he is unable to attend. He then presents a gift to the last headmaster, Ken Townsend, reminding everyone he was deputy for sixteen years, and then Ruth Thornhill, head of childcare and at the school for twenty-two years. Ken and Ruth are the longest-serving staff members still present at the school when it closes. As they ceremonially cut a specially baked cake together, Ken Bridge and his old teaching team look on and applaud.

While the weather is still bright, groups of friends make their way outside to the gardens in front of the hostel and the classrooms to take photographs. For me, it is the first time in eleven years I have seen these friends, and although we promise to keep in touch there is no guarantee this will happen, so we make the most of the moment.

This first picture is taken in front of the classrooms near the hostel and shows Gary Prescott, Jeff Garnett, Peter Dickinson, myself, David Powell, Thomas Howard and Christina Harrison. In the second picture we are joined by Leslie and Ruth Thornhill, their son Duncan and toddler daughter Claire.

Talking about the school closure, opinion is split. Many are angry and saddened at the policy that brought an end to Derby and other special schools; on the other hand, there are others glad to see the back of such institutions, with their roots in outdated Victorian ideals of taking a problem and hiding it away.

Although acknowledging the numerous happy memories, close camaraderie, achievements and good intentions of all at Derby School, living in a close-knit "artificial" world made integration back into the real world of adulthood and employment a major problem for me. I welcome the new enlightened policy and feel happy and reassured I will not be sending my children off to Preston.

As the afternoon draws to a close many of the ex-pupils want to keep the party going, still having much to talk about, so they decide to relocate to the Plungington pub just across the road. I am unable to attend as we have made plans to continue on for a weekend in Blackpool. We say

our farewells and take the bus back to Preston. I sincerely believe it will be the last time I ever visit the school.

But a school isn't just bricks and mortar, an institution

that policy can close. A school is more than the total of its parts and the most important part is the camaraderie of the people associated with that place. A band of individuals brought together by circumstance and adversity can have a strong bond and last down the years; this fellowship cannot be underestimated.

Little did I know it then, but Derby School would live on. Not as a special boarding school in Preston but taking a different form, as a dedicated group of friends who would remain in contact for many years to come. The next chapter brings the story up to date, chronicling the reunions and commitment of ex-staff and old school friends as they attempt to maintain the spirit and memory of Derby School. Throughout the 1990s and well into the new millennium, the pilgrimage is repeatedly made back to Preston as folk are determined to "Keep In Touch".

5

Keeping in Touch
1988–present

After the reunion of July 1988 the school finally closed its gates for the last time. There is a grand auction of all the books, equipment, bedding and furniture that had accumulated over the years. The buildings and offices of the school site are subsequently sold to various different businesses. They are inheriting some extremely well-maintained Victorian and post-war accommodation that will still be standing for many more years to come.

All activities of the Institute for Blind Welfare are transported to Howick House in Penwortham, at the other side of Preston (pictured below). This will now be their headquarters and base for all future operations.

The top original elementary school building on Lytham Road becomes offices of the accountants Wallwork, Nelson and Johnson, and can be seen floodlit at night. Ironically, these new owners blank out the "Blind Welfare" plaque that had caused such offence to the children for so many years, but now it is too late to make any difference.

The Roper Hostel and classrooms are transformed with a great deal of investment into Derby Lodge, a private home for the physically disabled of all ages. Downstairs, the hostel is redeveloped into community rooms, and upstairs the dormitories become several bedsits. The classrooms are altered and refurbished into self-contained flats for those inmates with more independence. The blind workshops, boiler house and laundry are boarded up and left empty and unsold.

These buildings have always been the most deprived of investment and maintenance and it appears at this time no one has the money or ambition to attempt any form of redevelopment. The gym also remains unused, awaiting a new purpose. The sports field is neglected and nature quickly takes over as it  becomes wild and overgrown. It has even been seen to have horses on it! [Keeping In Touch, 1, 1995]

As for ex-staff, life must continue, and for those who hadn't retired, alternative employment is needed. Ken

Townsend, the last headmaster, has several jobs during the first few years of the school's closure. First, he was an instructor at a Youth Training Scheme (YTS) centre, then a fundraiser for the Blackpool Blind Society and for a time drove a delivery van until he eventually settled in the position of support tutor at the University of Central Lancashire, based in Preston.

Ken Bridge, headmaster for over twenty years, retired in 1986, kept busy travelling round the district collecting money from the many charity boxes the Blind Welfare Society had placed around pubs and business in the local area, while making sure that it doesn't interfere with his other hobby of going on holiday. Since retiring, he has been on many exotic excursions, beginning with the Orient Express and then following that up with a round-the-world cruise. He also visited many far-flung countries like China, Singapore and Hong Kong.

Another former teacher enjoying his retirement is Morris Oakley. He occupies himself travelling round Europe in his camper van and riding his motorbike. He'd always been an enthusiastic biker. During his travels, he was lucky enough to be given the opportunity to drive a Great Western steam train [Keeping In Touch, 1, 2 & 3, 1995–1997].

Former Class 1 assistant and art teacher Jean Tomlinson continues to work for the Blind Welfare, now based at Howick House, and domestic science teacher Barbara Preston finds a job with the Lancashire Visually Handicapped Service [Keeping In Touch, 2, 1996].

Sheila Mintoft, former music teacher, swaps working in a boarding school, where the pupils imagined they were in prison, for a real prison! At Wymott Prison she teaches adult basic education to the "residents" and in her spare time enjoys badminton, tennis and of course music [Keeping In Touch, 3, 1997].

Leslie Thornhill is the only member of staff who continues to work at the old school site. The former housefather finds himself a position as assistant superintendent at Derby Lodge. His wife, Ruth, becomes a classroom assistant in a local junior school in Fulwood [Keeping In Touch, 2, 1996].

Three years on from the school closing, in November 1990 Margaret Thatcher quits as Prime Minister. The politician whom many blame for the school's demise stands down after her Cabinet refuse to back her in a second round of leadership elections. The Conservatives continue in power under new leader John Major, who succeeds five days later [http://news.bbc.co.uk/onthisday/hi/dates/stories/november/22/newsid, 2015].

While there are ex-pupils scattered all over Britain and abroad, the vast majority of ex-staff live and work around the Preston area, many using their previous employer the Preston and North Lancashire Blind Welfare Society as a hub for social activities. Howich House becomes a centre of communication and fellowship. Supported by the Penwortham charity and its director, Peter Taylor, a small network of ex-staff are able to gather, socialise and stay in contact.

In 1992, John Major stretches the Tories' winning streak to four general election victories in a row. It is an impressive feat, all the more startling as it had been pulled off against the backdrop of one of the worst recessions of the twentieth century. Major's victory confounded pollsters and pundits alike, many of whom had been predicting a hung parliament or an end to Labour's years in the wilderness [http://news.bbc.co.uk/1/hi/uk_politics/vote_2005/basics/4393317.stm. 2015].

At a gathering at Howick House in 1995, Ruth Thornhill, Jean Tomlinson and Barbara Preston have the joint inspiration to expand their social network to include ex-pupils and staff of Derby School and hold a grand reunion. To this end, they work on the administration with former secretary Mrs Dorothy Crean. Old school records are dug up and all preparations, including catering, are considered. Peter Taylor enthusiastically gives his support to the plans and makes freely available the resources and amenities of the Penwortham base as the event venue [Keeping In Touch, 1, 1995]. It is unfortunate the school itself can't be the focal point for such an occasion, but of course the property and grounds are now no longer owned by the charity.

During the summer of 1995, invitations are dispatched to as many ex-staff and pupils as there are contact details still available. The letter includes travel arrangements and a map, as most people invited will have no knowledge of Howick House or its location.

In this same year Microsoft launches its computer operating system Windows 95, beginning the revolution in home computers. It is still going to be many years before the Internet and social media are embraced by the general public, so communication and organisation of these reunions will be conducted by post and telephone for quite some time to come.

I remember coming in from the garden and taking a phone call from my old school friend Peter Dickinson, who lives in Preston, informing me of this first reunion. A few days later, I receive the letter. After losing contact with everyone from school after the last get-together in 1988, I am determined this time will be different. Peter offers to let me lodge with him over the weekend so we can have a good catch-up and look round Preston and Fulwood together.

I travel across the Pennines on Friday evening,

PRESTON & NORTH LANCASHIRE BLIND WELFARE SOCIETY

To All Staff and Ex-Pupils of Derby School, Preston.

You are invited to join ex-pupils/staff
for a DERBY SCHOOL
RE-UNION on
Saturday, 30th September, 1995
1 p.m. to 4.30 p.m.
at Howick House,
Howick Park Avenue,
Penwortham, Preston.
(Travel arrangements/map on separate sheet)
Light refreshments will be served.

If you are able to come along let us know, ring Mrs. Jean Tomlinson on 01772 744168 or complete the enclosed form and return it in the envelope provided. Ladies if you are married it would help if you let us have your maiden name as well as your married name.

If you are in contact with any one who went to Derby School please let them know about the re-union.

Helping local Blind people

and on Saturday morning before the reunion Peter and I visit the old school site. We catch the No. 23 Boys Lane bus up to Fulwood along Plungington Road from the bus station as we had often done during our days at Derby. Although we can't enter any of the buildings we are able to walk round the grounds and I take plenty of photographs. It is clear the new owners have put their stamp on the place. But that doesn't stop a multitude of memories returning to make me feel like a little boy all over again.

After a tour all round the grounds I become frustrated that we can't have a sneak peek inside, but to be honest we are trespassing on private property just standing on the drive so we are lucky to get that far. We have dinner at the Withy Trees pub before getting a taxi down the A59 to the reunion. We both arrive at about 2pm. I am familiar with Penwortham from my childhood; I used to stay weekends at Peter's home on Anchor Drive. Never did I expect to be returning twenty-four years later.

On Saturday 30th September 1995, from 1pm to 4.30pm at Howick House, the very first Derby School reunion since the school closed is held. The venue is very reminiscent of the Roper Hostel. The two buildings feel like they were built during the same era, the back end of the nineteenth century. The main room where the reunion is held reminds me of the school's dining hall; they are very similar. The main difference is the bright yellow handrails installed everywhere to assist the blind.

There is a great turnout of ex-pupils from all eras of the school's history; many I don't recognise, guests much older than me from the '50s and '60s and younger people who attended well after I had left. Peter and I eagerly search out recognisable faces from our time.

There are many teachers present from my time including Freda Shepherd, who is now married and called Wood, Morris Oakley, Linda Williams, Jean Mills, Jean Tomlinson, Chris Phillips, Ken Townsend and, arriving just after us, the main man himself, Ken Bridge. There are also teachers I don't recognise from after my time, like Barbara Preston and Julie Lewis.

It's surprising how intimidating my old teachers still are and I can't fully relax in their presence. I feel I must be on my best behaviour. The childcare department is very well represented with Miss Walsh, Mrs Neary, Mrs Clarkson, Mrs Brown, Mrs Cookson, and of course Leslie and Ruth

Thornhill. There are also many people I don't recognise and I have no idea if they are ex-pupils or staff. I find myself chatting mostly to Leslie Thornhill. This is surprising because while at school we never really got on, a clash of personalities, now he is clearly willing to let bygones be bygones and we enjoy discussing the past.

As the event draws to a close, Ken Townsend and Ken Bridge can't help but revert back to "teacher" mode to make speeches and be the centre of attention. The two ex-headmasters thank everyone for coming and Peter Taylor for his hospitality, and finally we are reminded that today is a happy coincidence marking the thirtieth anniversary of Ken Bridge starting at the school in 1965. It's also one hundred years since the Fulwood Blind Homes first opened and began this story.

I've had a great time meeting many old friends and exchanging contact details, this time promising to really keep in touch. I'm a little disappointed that more of my classmates haven't appeared, especially my old girlfriends, but I suspect most will have married and moved home, making the job of tracking them down difficult.

Here is a photograph from that first reunion showing four of my old friends: from left to right, David Powell,

Thomas Howard, Geraint Fawkes and Peter Dickinson. We were all together in Class 6 in 1975. David has come from nearby Chorley; Thomas from Heysham, near Morecambe; and Geraint from North Wales. Like me, Geraint is staying overnight; he is lodging with the Thornhills.

One very important new friend I have reacquainted myself with since the meeting in 1988 is Gary Prescott, whom I will meet up with many times to come in the future, brought together by our love of football and rugby league.

Sometime before the reunion, director Peter Taylor had suggested that a newsletter might be started to bring everyone up to date on what had transpired in the seven years since the school had closed. During the afternoon, it was agreed a committee be formed to produce this first newsletter.

A few weeks later, the first meeting of the newsletter committee is held, on 14th October 1995, at Howick House, where the name of "Keeping In Touch" was chosen. Writing in that first edition, Ken Bridge spoke about the first reunion:

'What a pleasure it was to meet again so many ex-pupils, staff and parents, especially those of you who had travelled long distances. There were surprises – who ever thought Brian Hilton would attend of his own free will? We never could obtain such success in his school days! But he certainly was an asset in helping us pay the telephone bills. There were shocks when, for instance, hearing of Kath (nee) Owen's fourteen-year-old son, I starkly became aware of my advancing years! I last saw Kathleen when she was sixteen years old. It was also noted that some of the male ex-pupils, like me, had expanded waistlines! The time passed quickly and my regret was that I didn't manage to chat to everyone before it was time to leave.' He went on to thank all those responsible for organising the reunion and said that the success of the whole event was a great tribute to their efforts. He finished by adding, 'It was a real "Derby Day" and we were all winners!'

The committee suggest that next year there should be a dinner dance or perhaps a hotel booked for the weekend and asked for feedback on these ideas. But their enthusiasm is not shared by the majority who are happy simply to repeat the trip to Penwortham. So it is settled that the next reunion will be at Howich House on Saturday 28th September 1996.

Thus begins a series of annual reunions and an associated "Keeping In Touch" newsletter produced by the Preston charity from information gathered at these get-togethers and sent out using updated contact details and content decided and edited by the committee. The members of this committee are a mixture of ex-staff and pupils all living close enough to gather at Penwortham regularly. Members include Ken Townsend and ex-students Kathleen Davies (née Owen), Steven Foster and Janet Troy. Appeals are made for stories and articles that can be included and readers are asked to post these to Jean Tomlinson

This begins the first significant exchange of information about the lives and careers of people associated with the school. For many, this is the first opportunity to discover how their classmates and associates are dealing with the grown-up world of employment and relationships. We are able to learn about friends who are now married with children, mates who went on to further education and even university, jobs and careers. I find it fascinating to

Derby School Reunions held at Preston and North Lancashire Blind Welfare Society, Howich House, Penwortham, Preston		
Order	Approximate number of attendees	Date
1st	No data	Saturday September 30th 1995
2nd	70	Saturday September 28th 1996
3rd	50	Saturday September 27th 1997
4th	50	Saturday September 25th 1999
5th	40	Sunday September 30th 2001
6th	60	Saturday September 28th 2002
7th	No data	Saturday September 27th 2003
8th	No data	September 2004
9th	No data	Saturday September 2005
10th	No data	September 2006
There were no reunions in 1998 and 2000.		

study the lives of others and compare them to my own. After gaining permission, telephone numbers are listed and school friends are able to communicate between each other without having to wait for the annual reunion. Many old friends are reconnected and arrange their own social events and get-togethers.

But not all the news is positive concerning achievement and success. There are many stories of frustration and despair over many years while attempting to gain a decent job, relationship breakdown, divorce and, for a small few, tragedy.

I have already mentioned in an earlier chapter my friend Ferenc, who died in February 1982. It now transpires he was just one of a small group of ex-pupils who, for one reason or another, were taken from us well before their time. That first newsletter lists them, from Stephen Gelling, who died in April 1981, to Vicky Swainbank just before that first meeting in July 1995. The others are Paul Shaw, Tracy McGuigan and Anthony Speight.

In the third issue of the newsletter it is stated that during the 1996 reunion a collection was made to enable a bouquet of flowers to be sent to Shirley Coulson, who lost her new baby and husband in the space of a few weeks earlier in the year. The information gathered during the publication of the "Keeping In Touch" newsletter was invaluable and I have referenced it regularly during the writing of this book.

1997 is a memorable year. First, ex-teacher Linda Williams married Jack Grant on Saturday May 3rd at Ampfield in Surrey. The "Keeping In Touch" newsletter reports that 'After a honeymoon in America (camping and backpacking) through Utah, Colorado, Dakota and Wyoming, the happy couple are now living in Walmer Bridge, Preston'.

Later the same month, Labour ends eighteen years in the political wilderness in spectacular style. The party returns to power with a parliamentary landslide, winning the biggest majority held by any government since 1935. Tony Blair's New Labour had gained a staggering 179-seat overall majority in the Commons as the Conservatives were tossed aside by the voters [http://news.bbc.co.uk/hi/english/static/vote2001/, 2015].

And in August we all wake to the shocking news of the death of Diana, Princess of Wales, in a car accident in a Paris tunnel. The accident happened after the princess left the Ritz Hotel in the French capital with her companion, Dodi Al Fayed – son of Harrods owner, Mohammed Al Fayed [http://news.bbc.co.uk/onthisday/hi/dates/stories/august/31/newsid, 2015]. A few weeks later, after the state funeral, Linda Grant (Williams) and her new husband attend that year's reunion. This is the first one I miss, and so do others. With only fifty people in attendance it is decided to miss a year before the next one. The reunions start again in 1999.

During the summer of 1998 we hear of the death of ex-domestic science teacher Barbara Preston, one of the original instigators of the reunions.

Over the years there is a core group of regulars. But every now and again a new face appears. Word slowly spreads and there is a small trickle of new attendees. One year, ex-teachers Ann Hilton and Ann Colbert arrive together. Peter Mounsey (childcare 1980–1987) and Mrs Walmsley make a visit. It is a shock to see the former confined to a wheelchair and looking so frail; when working at the school she was always such an intimidating figure.

I attend nearly all the reunions and each time this involves lodging with Peter Dickinson, who is kind enough to put me up on every occasion, first at his home in Preston and later when he moves to a terraced cottage in Longridge.

My visits become quite a tradition. The weekend always involved a night out round Preston, ending at a nightclub, usually "Legends" near the football ground. Later we go for a curry. Sometimes other friends, like Gary Prescott, join us. Always part of my plans is a trip to Fulwood. Peter and I  visit the old school, making note of the changes over the years. We walk up Black Bull Lane and call at old haunts like Boys Lane. We have a drink in the Plungington Hotel and reminisce about the school, which can be seen through the window.

While in discussion with Leslie Thornhill during one of the reunions, I mention my curiosity to see inside. After one particular get-together he offers me a lift up to Fulwood. Working at Derby Lodge he can gain access. He gives me a conducted tour upstairs and down of what was once the hostel. He takes me along the covered corridor outside the old classrooms which are now individual flats. It's over ten years since I last stepped inside the "school".

My most vivid memory of this visit is looking out of an upstairs window from the hostel across the gardens. Leslie points out the missing lamp post from the top of the steps. That old leaning lamp post had stood there like a drunken guardsman, ignored by all for so many years and now noticed because of its absence.

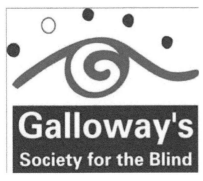

After the 1999 reunion it is decided to miss a year again and not have another until 2001. During this time, home computers and the Internet finally encroach on the world of Howich House. The blind charity receives an image makeover. In July 2000, the Blind Welfare becomes Galloway's Society for the Blind, named after William Wilding Galloway, a cotton merchant from Preston who left £40,000 to local charities, including £10,000 to the society, when he died in 1936. The society renamed itself to avoid its cumbersome previous name, which was commonly abbreviated to the ambiguous "The Blind Society", and to honour its greatest benefactor. Along with the change of name there is a new logo and website. This charity that started life over a hundred years ago in Preston's Corn Exchange now has a website and Internet presence [Wikipedia/Galloway's_Society_for_the_ Blind, 2015].

My regular visits to the old school site allow me to chronicle its development over the years. All the blind workshops are completely demolished and residential housing built in their place. This is a massive change in character for the area. Families are now living in modern flats between the old school yard and Cadley Brook, accessed from Derby Road. Gone are the white painted

football goalposts and cricket stumps; I feel like I've lost an old friend. The yard is a car park, and the steps leading from the yard to what was once the senior boys' end are also gone.

A year or so later, the old gym is developed into a ladies' fitness centre called Ladies Workout Express. This company, specialising in thirty-minute workouts for women of all ages, refurbishes the premises.

As the new millennium dawns, the potential of the computer and how it can aid the visually impaired and many other disabilities is becoming clear. I fully embrace this new technology and its power to change lives. It almost feels like a natural progression from the typewriting lessons we took at Derby. I enrol on a computer course in Wakefield and soon gain new qualifications in information technology.

In 2001, the newsletter announces the tragic death of Ken Bridge. This comes as quite a shock because we had no knowledge of any prior illness, but the last reunion was two years ago and, of course, much can happen in that time. Going to these reunions in the 1990s and meeting so many

ex-members of staff – teachers and childcare – I can't fail to notice the respect and admiration everyone has for Ken. He had such a positive influence on so many people.

Just looking at my own case, it was Ken who first encouraged my independence by giving me my "privileges" and then putting my name forward to compere the Christmas show for two years. Later, I was in the all-conquering Young Farmers Quiz team and, finally, it was Ken who during my last year encouraged me to travel home alone. At first, it was difficult for me to settle down at Derby and I was often in trouble. Ken was the authoritarian figure to fear rather than admire, handing out the punishment. But as I grew up I came to appreciate his guiding, encouraging and supporting influence.

Although the death of Ken Bridge is a major topic at that year's reunion, there is the shadow of a far greater disaster hanging over proceedings. Just nineteen days earlier on the morning of 11th September 2001, nineteen hijackers take control of four commercial passenger jets flying out of airports on the east coast of the United States. Two of the aircraft are deliberately flown into the Twin Towers of the World Trade Centre in New York, with a third hitting the Pentagon in Virginia. The fourth plane never reaches its intended target, crashing in Pennsylvania. The total loss of life on 9/11 is nearly 3,000. It is the worst loss of life due to a terrorist incident on US soil [http://www.bbc.co.uk/history/events/the_september_11th_terrorist_attacks, 2015].

At the reunion, a letter from Mary Henessy (ex-pupil) is read out to everyone. In this letter she suggests that a seat or tree be bought and named in Ken's memory, as he had touched the lives of so many people in so many different ways [Galloway's Society newsletter, 2001]. The newsletter asks for anyone who wishes to contribute towards a garden seat or tree to be located at Galloway's to please send donations to Jean Tomlinson.

In 2002, historic Preston wins the coveted prize of Golden City status, beating off a challenge from twenty-six other English contenders. The town, which calls itself "Proud Preston", wins the contest, drawn up as part of the Queen's Golden Jubilee year to celebrate  her fifty years on the throne [http://news.bbc.co.uk/1/hi/england/1872505.stm, 2015].

It becomes the first new English city since Brighton and Hove and Wolverhampton were given the status to mark the new millennium, two years ago. In August, the Ken Bridge Memorial Fund closes, raising £350.

The main aim of the September 2002 reunion is to dedicate a seat to the memory of Ken Bridge. Ken's sister Elsie and her family, along with his lifelong friend Mrs Evelyn Brooks, are invited to the short ceremony. Ex-'50s pupil and houseparent Graham Crawshaw attends his first reunion and finds he is the only person from those early years present. Ken Townsend opens the proceedings with his three outstanding memories of Ken. Much of this speech is a repeat of what he said at Ken's retirement party in 1986. A teacher representative, Freda Wood (Shepherd), then speaks about how Ken changed the school for the better. Mrs Mary Neary, then from childcare, speaks of the changes he made to the social areas. Finally, Mary Henessy, whose original idea it was, speaks about how Ken changed lots of things at the school from the viewpoint of the children. We then all go outside. The bench is carried over to a corner of the Howich House gardens where it is to remain. A bronze plate is unveiled with the inscription –

In memory of
Ken Bridge
Head Teacher Derby School, Preston
1965–1986

Many people then take the opportunity to sit on the seat and have their photographs taken. £210 is passed on to Peter Taylor Director of Galloway's so that plants around the seat area can be purchased and renewed. One of my favourite memories of Ken Bridge was when he taught us senior boys how to make curry on Saturday evenings.

This began my life-long love of curry and I still make it to Ken's recipe today. He was one of the main attractions at the reunions and helped pay for the catering, so his loss is felt on many levels. From this point on, interest in the Penwortham gatherings begins to wane.

After two years of computer and IT training, the confidence and qualifications gained enable me to take an FE teaching certificate at Leeds University and I start work as an IT tutor at Leeds College of Technology. Just one example of how computers, with their accessibility functions like changing text size, increasing zoom and spell checker, can make such a massive difference to performance and achievement. Together with programs like Microsoft Office, there is finally hope of levelling the playing field for the visually impaired.

I continue to visit Preston in the hope of seeing new faces and I am not disappointed. Finally, after many years, one of my old girlfriends, Kathleen Allison, makes an appearance. I also begin discussions with Graham Crawshaw, who is writing a book about his life and struggle to gain fulfilling employment while visually impaired. His book talks about his time in the 1950s at the School for the Partially Sighted, Preston, and later when he returned as a houseparent in 1973.

He has carried out much research about the origins of the school and been assisted by Freda Wood (Shepherd) and Ken Townsend. I find the idea of writing a book very exciting and we arrange to meet in Leeds for a drink and further discuss his work. I buy a copy of Graham's book, "A Partial View", 2005, and decide to write my own book, but rather than my life story I will write about the school using Graham's research as a starting point.

Galloway's heavily invests in new computer technology and open an IT training room. With the aid of specialist software Dragon and Supernova, the blind and visually impaired are now able to learn IT skills to aid employability. After the 2006 reunion it is decided not to hold a reunion in 2007 but to have one last grand event in 2008 which will mark twenty years since the school closed. But this get-together never materialises, so the very last reunion is 2006; but sadly, the guests gathered didn't know that at the time.

Over the course of these reunions nearly every living member of staff who worked at Derby made an appearance. In an age before social media these events were the only method of reconnecting with lost friends and acquaintances from the past. It was also a valuable vehicle for discussion and reflection regarding the school and its impact and place in people's lives.

Over the eleven years that these events are staged there is one major character in the story of Derby School missing, and the impact of his absence is felt ever greater because of his popularity. George Lambert Gooch made a massive contribution to the school. In addition to being a form tutor and science teacher, he was the school pianist, Christmas show lighting and sound engineer, weekend child supervisor and organiser of countless after-school activities. He also took groups for days out to Southport,

Morecambe and Blackpool. There can't be many who could have invested more of their own time to the life of Derby School than him. Probably the most liked, remembered and respected teacher. Yet he never appeared at any of the reunions, not even the 1988 final Open Day. Originating from Norwich, he lived at the school for fifteen years then purchased a house in Much Hoole, Preston, in 1980. He lived nearby and would have known about these gatherings. So his absence will always be a mystery. Then, in 2006, I learn of his death. It wasn't till I visited Mary Neary in 2010 that I am informed he took his own life, a really sad and tragic end for a teacher who gave so much to the school [M. Neary, 2010].

There was evidently a need for people to come together at these reunions. I suspect the majority of ex-staff saw these events as simply a great social occasion, but for the ex-pupils it was far more. Certainly, socialising came into it, but it was also about discussing with others the shared issues of being a boarder at a special school and living with a visual impairment. For the first time, many could talk to others with similar experiences and problems, no longer alone.

Today, this community is online. Ex-pupils have set up their own Derby School Group page on Facebook. Talking to each other is only a few clicks away and get-togethers are organised in Nottingham, Sheffield and Manchester in just minutes. How Dorothy Crean and Jean Tomlinson would have loved this technology when first trying to contact people for those early reunions.

After decades of isolation, now via Facebook everyone can be connected. In conjunction with email and text

messages, the entire life of the school can be discussed, and if anyone wants a tour of the old school site all they need do is access Google Street View. Isn't technology amazing?

Today, all the main school buildings are still occupied and in use by different businesses. Derby Lodge, the residential care home that took over the hostel and classrooms in 1989, is still operating from this site. Up the hill, various different sections of the main building, now called Derby House, have seen a variety of owners over the years, including the charity Barnardo's and a commercial insurance and risk management firm. The gym is currently occupied by "Just for Ladies", an inchloss boot camp.

The original blind charity that first set up the school is still going strong as Galloway's Society for the Blind, now based in Penwortham, Morecambe, Chorley and Southport. They continue to support people living with blindness or a visual impairment across the west of Lancashire. From four regional centres, they provide vital help and services. The charity has been remodelled to the needs of the modern age with a new look website and Facebook page. This year, 2017, it celebrates its 150th anniversary [www.galloways. org.uk/, 2015].

Today, this charity is the only existing organisation that links back directly to the Fulwood Blind Homes, the blind workshops and the Derby School, to a time when children with a disability were segregated from their friends and family, taken away from all that was familiar, and "sent to Preston".

Author's Notes

I was nine years old when I was "Sent to Preston". I had grown up hearing my mother told by the experts that I should be sent away to a special school for a better chance in life. Every appointment at the hospital ended with a doctor explaining I needed a specialist education. Nevertheless, no further action was ever taken.

I'd learnt to ignore all the talk and speculation, so when the day finally arrived and I found myself miles away from home and all that was familiar, standing alone on the driveway of a strange little boarding school in Lancashire, I was confused and traumatised. My mind was spinning with so many questions. Why did I need to go to a special school? Why was it so far away that I needed to stay there? Why wasn't there a school like this nearer home? Why Preston of all places? At the time I needed to focus on my immediate situation, learning to cope and acclimatise to a completely new way of life; this totally overwhelmed me. But the questions never disappeared.

I've always been interested in history and while at Leeds University taking my Certificate in Education I learnt about research and writing assignments. About the same time I met Graham Crawshaw and after reading his book decided that if I expanded on his initial research and wrote my own book, I could finally investigate the answers to my questions.

157

Those simple questions have been the driving force of my book and I think I have answered them. It's been a very personal journey finding the answers, and great therapy. I feel much happier now I can finally explain the historical events that took me from home to Preston in 1970.

My research has mainly come from Graham's book, the Internet and talking to ex-pupils via social media. Leeds University taught me to put everything into historical context and always refer to the relevant Act of Parliament, which is where most changes in thinking and policy begin.

My story isn't complete. There are gaps in some areas of research, but I've been compiling this book for many years and have to call it a day at some point. There will be people who are familiar with the subject who note that a certain person or event is not mentioned. I'm sorry, but this story spans over a century and a half of British educational history and I can't mention or know about everyone or everything. This book is mainly to give the unfamiliar a taste of what a special boarding school for the visually impaired was like, not a document that chronicles every single event.

When I was a child I loved to make scrap books. I have tried to make this book as visually interesting as possible using plenty of photographs and graphics.

Unfortunately, much of my story is from a boy's point of view. I have included as much input from ex-Derby schoolgirls as possible. Boys outnumbered girls by three to one, and the only other ex-pupil to write a book about the school is also male. We were strictly segregated during my time; as a result, I have little knowledge of what life was like at the school for a girl. Maybe one day another book will be written from the female perspective.

Both my daughters have a visual impairment and attended mainstream schools with statements of special educational needs. I was so happy and relieved they didn't suffer the trauma of being sent away. Although I have much fondness for Derby School, I am thankful these special schools are now a thing of the past and only exist in the history books.

Garry Cheesbrough, 10th February 2015

Appendix

This is my own personal progress at Derby School. It demonstrates the unique system by which pupils moved through the classes. I spent over two terms in Class 3 before moving up each year, until reaching the top class at thirteen and then remaining in that class for three years. Each child had a unique journey through the school depending on their yearly exam results.

Class	Terms Attended	Age	Teacher	Accommodation
Class 3	April 1970 – July 1970	9.5 – 9.8	George Gooch	Intermediate Boys
Class 3	September 1970 – July 1971	9.10 – 10.8	George Gooch	Intermediate Boys
Class 3	September 1971 – July 1972	10.10 – 11.8	George Gooch	Intermediate Boys
Class 4	September 1972 – July 1973	11.10 – 12.8	Ann Colbert	Intermediate Boys
Class 5	September 1973 – July 1974	12.10 – 13.8	Ann Hilton	Intermediate Boys

Class 6	September 1974 – July 1975	13.10 – 14.8	Ken Townsend	Senior Boys
Class 6	September 1975 – July 1976	14.10 – 15.8	Ken Townsend	Senior Boys
Class 6	September 1976 – May 1977	15.10 – 16.6	Ken Townsend	Senior Boys

Here are the results of my internal examinations while in Class 3. My rapid progress can be clearly seen. I arrive at Derby School with "below average intelligence", as quoted from my first school report. In the first exam I finish next to last with 39%. Two years later, I move up to fourth position with 75%. That result allows me to move up to Class 4.

Order	Date	Position (15 in class)	%
1st	July 1970	14th	39
2nd	Jan 1971	11th	50
3rd	July 1971	13th	44
4th	July 1972	4th	75

Teachers at the School for the Partially Sighted, from 1965 the Derby School, Preston

Headmasters
Fred Rothwell 1945–1965
And Class 4 Remedial
Ken Bridge 1965–1986
Ken Townsend 1986–1988

Deputy Headmasters
Donald Taysum 1945–1970
And Class 6
Ken Townsend 1970–1986
And Class 6 1970–1986, renamed Class 8 in 1980, and English

Teachers
Beryl Ryding (Class 1)
Miss Littlewood (Class 1) – 1957
Freda Shepherd (Wood) 1957–1985 (Class 1, renamed Class 2 in 1980)
Jean Tomlinson 1971–1988 (Class 1 assistant)
Alice Smith 1945–1961 (Class 2)
Miss Goodwin 1961–1964 (Class 2)
Mrs Best 1964–1967 (Class 2)
Miss Ludden 1967–1968 (Class 2)
Linda Williams 1968–1988 (Class 2, renamed Class 3 in 1980)

Jean Mills 1968–1988 (Class 2A, renamed Class 2 in 1980)
John Law – 1955 (Class 3)
Evelyn Webb (Taysum) 1955–1957 (Class 3)
Brain Turner 1957–1966 (Class 3)
Ann Colbert 1966–1967 (Class 3) and 1967–1974 (Class 4)
George Lambert Gooch 1965–1967 (Class 4 Remedial)
1967–1988 (Class 3, renamed Class 4 in 1980)
Mr Hobday – 1974
Mr Worsdale (Class 4, renamed Class 5 in 1980)
Edwin Lees '50s (Class 5)
Noel Jones '50s (Class 5)
John Robinson – 1970 (Class 5)
Anne Hilton 1970–1975 (Class 5)
Chris Phillips 1975–1982 (Class 5, 7 and Maths)
Julie Lewis (Wright) (Class 5 and Science)
Mrs Clay (Class 8 and English) 1986-1988
Mrs Walmsley 1980s (Class 6 and Art)
Linda Brindle (Class 7 and Maths) 1982–1988
Morris Oakley (PE) 1971–1986
Sheila Mintoft (Music)
Mrs Booth 1970s (Typing)
Mrs de Santo 1980s (Typing)
Barbara Preston (Domestic Science) 1980–1988

Acknowledgements

A Chronological Survey of Work for the Blind (supplement). Compiled by Mary G. Thomas, (formerly Information Officer, Royal National Institute for the Blind, published for the Royal National Institute for the Blind, Great Portland Street, London by Sir Isaac Pitman & Sons, Ltd, London. First published 1953

Madeleine Dean (1987). The story of the Institute for the Blind Welfare and School for the Partially Sighted, unpublished report available from the Local Studies Loan Collection, Lancashire County Library HQ, Preston

Lancashire Evening Post, 1945
Lancashire Evening Post, Singleton. E., 1996
Lancashire Evening Post, Alker R., 1987

"A Partial View" by Robert Graham Crawshaw. First published 2005

"Keeping In Touch" Ex-staff and pupils' newsletter. Compiled and edited by the Newsletter Committee, published 1995–2006

An Introduction to Children with Special Educational Needs, Second Edition, M. Alcott, 2002

Websites

www.henshaws.org.uk/about/our-history.aspx, 2010
www.lep.co.uk/news/opinion, 2010
www.stvin.com, 2011
www.spartacus.schoolnet.co.uk, 2011
www.wikipedia.org/wiki/Second_Boer_War, 2011
www.britannia.com/history/nar20hist5.html, 2011
www.ribi.org/about-us/what-is-rotary, 2011
http://jim.leeder.users. What is PSS? 2011
http://en.wikipedia.org/wiki/Three-Day_Week, 2011
www.strike84.co.uk, 2011
www.bbc.co.uk/britishstylegenius, 2014
http://www.galloways.org.uk, 2014
http://news.bbc.co.uk/1/hi/england/1872505.stm, 2015
http://news.bbc.co.uk/onthisday/hi/dates/stories/
november/22/newsid, 2015
http://www.bbc.co.uk/history/events/the_
september_11th_terrorist_attacks, 2015

Main Facebook Contributors

Llewellyn Sadler 1950–1958
David S Rowland 1955–1961
Eileen M Berrisford 1964–1969
John Blain 1968–1973
Susan Elizabeth Kendrick (née Davis) 1968–1979
Paul Barnfather 1978–1982
Liz Minton (daughter of first Deputy Head Donald Taysum)

Other Contributors

Michael Hartley 1947–1952
Mary Neary 1961–1981

Kathleen Davies (nee Owen) 1969–1973
Jill Ryan (nee Unsworth) 1973–1976
Gary Prescott 1968–1979
Steven Foster 1970–1979
Ferenc Schmidt 1972–1977 (communication with his
parents in 1995)

Video references
We're Not Blind, BBC Schools programme Scene, first
broadcast 1975
Christmas Show, 1983
BBC Northwest Tonight (broadcast April 1986)
Sports Day, July 1986
Ken Bridge's Retirement Party, July 1986
Last Open Day, July 1988

Thanks to Galloway's Society for the Blind and special
thanks to Peter Taylor.

Thanks ,Terri, for all the love and support.

If you want to know more about this subject please watch
"We're Not Blind" BBC documentry.